EMPIRICISM
AND SUBJECTIVITY

European Perspectives

European Perspectives
A Series in Social Thought and Cultural Criticism
Lawrence D. Kritzman, Editor

European Perspectives presents outstanding books by leading European thinkers. With both classic and contemporary works, the series aims to shape the major intellectual controversies of our day and to facilitate the tasks of historical understanding.

For a complete list of books in the series, see pages 165–66.

EMPIRICISM
AND SUBJECTIVITY

AN ESSAY ON
HUME'S THEORY OF HUMAN NATURE

GILLES DELEUZE

Translated and with an Introduction by
CONSTANTIN V. BOUNDAS

COLUMBIA UNIVERSITY PRESS
NEW YORK

Columbia University Press wishes to express its
appreciation for assistance given by the government
of France through Le Ministère de la Culture in
the preparation of this translation.

COLUMBIA UNIVERSITY PRESS
Publishers Since 1893
NEW YORK   CHICHESTER, WEST SUSSEX

Copyright © 1991 Columbia University Press
Empirisme et Subjectivité. Essai sur la Nature Humaine selon Hume
Copyright © 1953 Presses Universitaires de France

Library of Congress Cataloging-in-Publication Data

Deleuze, Gilles.
[Empirisme et subjectivité. English]
Empiricism and subjectivity / an essay on Hume's theory of human
nature / Gilles Deleuze ; translated and with an introduction by
Constantin V. Boundas.
p.   cm. —
Translation of: Empirisme et subjectivité.
Includes bibliographical references and index.
ISBN 978-0-231-06813-0
1. Hume, David, 1711-1775. Treatise of human nature. I.Title
II. Series.
B1489.D413   1991
128—dc20   90-26497

Columbia University Press books are
printed on permanent and
durable acid-free paper

Printed in the United States of America
10 9 8 7 6 5 4 3

TO JEAN HYPPOLITE
A SINCERE AND RESPECTFUL HOMAGE

CONTENTS

PREFACE TO THE ENGLISH-LANGUAGE EDITION

WE DREAM SOMETIMES of a history of philosophy that would list only the new concepts created by a great philosopher—his most essential and creative contribution. The case of Hume could begin to be made with the following list:

—He established the concept of *belief* and put it in the place of knowledge. He laicized belief, turning knowledge into a legitimate belief. He asked about the conditions which legitimate belief, and on the basis of this investigation sketched out a theory of *probabilities*. The consequences are important: if the act of thinking is belief, thought has fewer reasons to defend itself against error than against *illusion*. Illegitimate beliefs perhaps inevitably surround thought like a cloud of illusions. In this respect, Hume anticipates Kant. An entire art and all sorts of rules will be required in order to distinguish between legitimate beliefs and the illusions which accompany them.

—He gave the *association* of ideas its real meaning, making it a practice of cultural and *conventional* formations (conventional instead of contractual), rather than a theory of the human mind. Hence, the association of ideas exists for the sake of law, political economy, aesthetics, and so on. People ask, for example, whether it is enough to shoot an arrow at a site in order to become its owner, or whether one should touch the spot with one's own hand. This is a question about the correct association between a person and a thing, for the person to become the owner of the thing.

—He created the first great logic of *relations*, showing in it that all relations (not only "matters of fact" but also relations among ideas) are external to their terms. As a result, he constituted a multifarious world of experience based upon the principle of the exteriority of relations. We start with atomic parts, but these atomic parts have transitions, passages, "tendencies," which circulate from one to another. These tendencies give rise to *habits*. Isn't this the answer to the question "what are we?" We are habits, nothing but habits—the habit of saying "I." Perhaps, there is no more striking answer to the problem of the Self.

We could certainly prolong this list, which already testifies to the genius of Hume.

Gilles Deleuze 1989

TRANSLATOR'S ACKNOWLEDGMENTS

I AM INDEBTED to Jacqueline Code, Allison van Rooy, and Réal Fillion for their invaluable help with earlier drafts of this translation. Susan Dyrkton, as she has done so often before, gave me her sound editorial advice and her friendship, and I am grateful for both gifts. To Marg Tully, probably the most frequently acknowledged typist in the Academy and certainly one among the most deserving acknowledgment, a sincere expression of thanks. The completion of the present translation was greatly facilitated by a sabbatical leave granted me by Trent University during the academic year 1989–1990, and I am thankful for it. I am also grateful to Professors François Laruelle and Anne-Françoise Schmid-Laruelle for their hospitality in Paris, and for the time they so kindly spent with me, without which my understanding of the rhizome named "Deleuze" and of the articulations of the sprawling philosophies of difference would have been much poorer than they are now. Above all, to Linda Carol Conway, who effortlessly knows how to build with childhood blocks and how to become like everybody else, until we meet again, a heartfelt "thank you."

EMPIRICISM
AND SUBJECTIVITY

DELEUZE, EMPIRICISM, AND THE STRUGGLE FOR SUBJECTIVITY

I

Every history of philosophy has its chapter on empiricism. . . . But in Hume there is something very strange which completely displaces empiricism, giving it a new power, a theory and practice of relations, of the AND. . . .

—Gilles Deleuze–Claire Parnet, *Dialogues*

THE THEORY AND politics of paratactic discourse, or of the minor stuttering in one's own language to which these lines allude, are likely to evoke today [1990] the adventures of *The Logic of Sense* (1969), the assemblages of *Kafka: Toward a Minor Literature* (1975), and the body without organs of the *A Thousand Plateaus* (1980). But in fact the quotation implicates a much earlier segment of the Deleuzian diagram of this discourse, inscribed with the name of Hume, and this implication has yet to receive the attention it deserves. It seems likely that a mindful consideration of this segment, in conjunction perhaps with the segment-Bergson[1] and the segment-Leibniz,[2] may begin to pay attractive dividends toward a more accurate charting of Deleuze's nomadic image of thought. Next to the literary, linguistic, and psychoanalytic bodies of *délire*, recently unveiled by Jean-Jacques Lecercle,[3] a philosophical body will then begin to take shape, and Deleuze's reasons for having assiduously tended to it over the last thirty-six years will emerge progressively into a stronger light.

One of his last books in circulation today to be translated into English, *Empiricism and Subjectivity* is Deleuze's second in a long list of book-length publications, initiated in 1952 and still being augmented at regular intervals.[4] This small book appeared in the Collection "Epiméthée" of the Presses Universitaires de France in 1953. One year before, in collaboration with André Cresson, Deleuze had released in the "Collection Philosophes" of the same house another book entitled *David Hume: Sa Vie, son oeuvre, avec un exposé de sa philosophie.* In one of its chapters, "Complément sur l'oeuvre," today's reader can easily recognize Deleuze's pen at work in the construction of a less elaborate version of the elegant discussion of Hume which was going to be deployed, within one year, in *Empiricism and Subjectivity.* In 1972, Deleuze returns to Hume in a chapter-long contribution to the *Histoire de la philosophie,* then edited by François Châtelet on behalf of Hachette Littérature.[5] One can find here a much abbreviated version of the 1953 book, but with no significant departure from any of the major points of its extended argument.

To this day, Deleuze has not revisited Hume, with the exception of some reminiscing references to his own earlier writings,[6] made often in the context of "the thought of the Outside" which has always fascinated him and informed his rhizomatic theory and practice. Hume is curiously absent from the series of memories/tributes of the *One Thousand Plateaus,*[7] to the point that an *argumentum e silentio* could be made, suggesting that a youthful enthusiasm with Hume had faded away. But such an argument, I think, would be missing the point, for the intensity named "Hume" has not ceased to resonate throughout Deleuze's writings. Named or not, the intensive encounter with Hume gave Deleuze a decisive and unbending preference for empiricism against all forms of transcendental philosophy. Acknowledged or not, the empiricist principle of difference, along with the theorem of the externality of all relations[8] which was derived from it, strengthened Deleuze's choice of minoritarian discourse[9] and fed into the problematic of paratactic serializations.[10] Finally, whether marked or unmarked, the resources of Hume consolidated Deleuze's opposition to the *petitio principii* of all theories endowing the transcendental field with the very subjective (egological and personological) coordinates the constitution of which should rather be accounted for and explained. The same resources "motivated" Deleuze's relentless quest for an "activated" and mind-transcending subject whose pathways would avoid the transcendental turn.[11]

II

The concept exists just as much in empiricism as in rationalism, but it has a completely different nature: it is a being-multiple, instead of being-one, a being-whole or being as subject. Empiricism is fundamentally linked to a logic—a logic of multiplicities (of which relations are only one aspect).

—Gilles Deleuze, Preface to the English
Language Edition of the *Dialogues*

The determination of Deleuze's place in the mindscape of the new French theory will always require complex and delicate negotiations; that his place, though, is prominent in it is not under dispute. It is therefore strange to observe that the frequently noticed new French theoretical bend toward empiricism has not yet generated discussions worthy of the intense interest in it by one of its leading contributors. Even Deleuze's reiteration of his continuing allegiance to empiricism made in the Preface to the English Language Edition of his *Dialogues* with Claire Parnet has not lifted the silence.[12]

Nevertheless, signposts, indicating that empiricism has been more than a whimsical choice in the post-structuralist range of options, are not lacking. For example, in V. Descombes's helpful compendium of *Modern French Philosophy* one finds a reference to Deleuze's project as a "search for a Transcendental Empiricism," together with the claim that, for Deleuze, philosophy is either dialectical or empiricist, "according to whether the difference between concept and intuition . . . is taken to be a conceptual or a non-conceptual difference."[13] Derrida's sibylline reference to empiricism as "the dream of a purely *heterological* thought at its source" is also well known. Indeed this reference is important enough to justify a more faithful reproduction: "[Empiricism is a] *pure* thought of *pure* difference. . . . We say the *dream* because it must vanish at *daybreak*, as soon as language awakens." "But perhaps," continues Derrida, "one will object that it is language which is sleeping. Doubtless, but then one must, in a certain way, become classical once more, and again find other grounds for the divorce between speech and thought. *This route is quite, perhaps too, abandoned today.*"[14] These lines were written in 1967; Descombes repeated them in 1979.[15] I have often wondered why the alternative route, created by Deleuze in 1953, was not kept open or traveled more frequently.

Truth to tell, a few commentators did make the point that the new French theoretical interest in empiricism indicates an active search for a ground which, unlike transcendental fields, would be hospitable to rhizomatic synapses and diagrammatic displacements.[16] But no one matched Deleuze's ability to seize this interest and to turn it into a war machine against the verities and the evidences constituting the object of the famous [conscious] phenomenological gaze. In assembling this war machine, Deleuze mobilized all those who, along with Lucretius, Hume, Spinoza, Nietzsche, and Bergson, share "a secret bond formed by the critique of the negative, the culture of joy, the hatred of interiority, the externality of forces and relations, and the denunciation of power . . ."[17] In this context, Deleuze has often confessed his low tolerance for the scholastic tactics of phenomenology which enshrine common and good sense.[18] In more argumentative moments—in *The Logic of Sense*, for instance—encounters with Husserl fueled a sustained critique of phenomenology, exposing the latter's fixation on the evidences of consciousness, its fatal surrender to the doxic element of common and good sense, and above all, the fraudulent duplication of the empirical domain by a transcendental field endowed with personal and egological dimensions. According to Deleuze, these dimensions still represent phenomenology's unreduced and uncritical presuppositions.[19]

Of course, Deleuze's war machine, mounted on empiricist lines and aimed at phenomenology (or hermeneutics) is not fueled with unmitigated invective. Husserl is not exactly treated like a schoolboy in *The Logic of Sense*, nor can one easily overlook Deleuze's powerful and elegant phenomenological descriptions in the essay on Michel Tournier, even if those descriptions, in the long run, are made to stand on their heads.[20] The elucidation of the struggles for subjectivity in Deleuze's later works, built as they are around the notions "fold" and "folding," has clear and acknowledged connections with Heidegger (*Zwiefalt*) and Merleau-Ponty (*pli, plissement*).[21] Tempting, though, as it may be—and even fashionably ecumenical[22]—I would not want to interpret these gestures as indications of a Deleuzian program for the radicalization of phenomenology. The radicalization of phenomenology, Deleuze-style, amounts to the transformation of phenomenology (and not only of a "vulgar" intentionalist reflection of it) into an ontology of intensive forces, extended forms, and of the "folding" or "internalization" of these forces and forms. And neither intensive forces nor the "fold" are phenomena, "sensa," or cogitationes.[23]

The transition from phenomenology to nomadic sensation and thought finds its mature moment in Deleuze's enlisting Bergson in the cause of radical empiricism.[24] According to Deleuze, Bergson, having questioned the privilege of natural perception and the subordination of movement to poses, creates the possibilities for an investigation of the "nonhuman" or "superhuman" originary world wherein images move and collide in a state of universal variation and undulation. This is a world with no axes, no centers, no ups or downs. In his quest for the pure perception (the *sentiendum*), Bergson breaks with the philosophic tradition which had assigned light to the mind and conceived consciousness as a searchlight summoning things up from their essential darkness. Unlike phenomenology, which remained faithful to this tradition, Bergson's vision solicited things in the context of their own luminosity. As for consciousness, instead of being the light of the old image of thought, it is, for Bergson, an opaque blade without which light would go on diffusing itself forever, never reflected and ever revealed. Deleuze subscribes to all these claims and also to Bergson's characterization of conscious perception as the object perceived, *minus* the aspects of it which do not interest the perceiver. Bergson and Deleuze, therefore, join hands in their demand that consciousness be constituted. Beginning with the *Abgrund* of an Empedoclean world of elements, consciousness must be exposed as the center, the obstacle, and the "living image" which blocks and reflects the light-lines hitherto diffused in evry possible direction. Deleuze's later texts will reiterate this demand, and they will designate subjectivity as the "fold" which bends and envelops the forces of the Outside.[25]

This choice of empiricism over phenomenology in the context of a new and more critical image of thought is bound to be resisted by some, although the resistance, I suspect, will be based on a more traditional access to empiricism, markedly different from that of Deleuze. We will do well to remember that for Deleuze philosophical *mathesis* has little to do with purported solutions or answers and everything to do with the question and the problem, or the ability of the problem to coordinate or serialize other questions within its range of tonalities.[26] Viewed from this perspective, the textbook definition of empiricism, which attributes to experience the origin *and* the source of validity of all possible knowledge, is, in fact, an answer without a question. Strictly speaking, the definition is not even plausible, because, despite what the definition implies, knowledge does not represent the primary concern of the empiricists, nor does experience play the kind of constitutive role that textbooks assign to it. Knowledge is not primary. Deleuze reminds us that Hume was primarily a moralist, a historian, and a political philosopher who placed his epistemology in the service of these concerns. Knowledge is possible because our passions provide our ideas with associative links in view of our actions and ends. The practical interest, being primary, activates the theoretical interest, and raises sooner or later the delicate issue of how to harmonize nature and human nature. What is often overlooked in our discussions of empiricism is that experience is not unambiguously constitutive. For if by "experience" we mean atomic and distinct perceptions, the relations which associate these perceptions to each other, creating thereby an aura of belief and anticipation, cannot be accounted for. This is because, in the opinion of Deleuze, Hume views relations as the effects of the principles of human nature; he does not attempt to derive them from our experience of atomic and distinct perceptions. Or again if by "experience" we mean the sum total of our observations hitherto, general rules and principles will not be accounted for, precisely because they themselves constitute experience and cannot therefore be derived from it. Hence, a definition of empiricism, which does not first problematize the nature and status of experience, is of little value.[27]

A more helpful definition of empiricism, in Deleuze's estimate, must respect the irreducible dualism that exists between things and relations, atoms and structure, perceptions and their causes, *and also* relations and their causes. Viewed from this vantage point, empiricism will be the theory of the externality of relations, and conversely, all theories which entail the derivation of relation from the nature of things would be resolutely nonempiricist. In the last analysis, Deleuze's commitment to empiricism rests on his conviction that relations are syntheses whose provenance cannot be explained on the basis of the representationalist matrix idea/atom or mind/collection of atoms. Relations are the effect of the principles of human nature and the latter, as we shall see, constitute the subject at the same time that they constitute relations.[28]

Thus, Deleuze's essay shows empiricism to be marked by an irreducible dualism between things and relations, and claims to capture thereby the sense of Hume's dual strategy of atomism (the different, the disparate) and associationism (*mise en série, parataxis.*) For if atomism "is the theory of ideas insofar as relations are external to them, and associationism, the theory of relations insofar as they are external to ideas, that is, insofar as they depend on (the principles of human nature),"[29] Hume, instead of pulverizing the given, as his critics often allege, would have embarked upon the study of the mechanism which allows atoms to fit in a structure. As long as the mind is a collection of atoms in motion, and mover and motion indistinguishable from each other, and as long as the mind can be likened to moving images without a frame to restrict their movement, Hume can easily show that atomism is not a sufficient condition for the constitution of a science of humanity. This science can be constituted only after the naturalization of the mind as the result of the operation of associative principles upon it—in other words, only after the constitution of the subject inside the mind as the product of principles of human nature transcending the mind.

Now, the reasons why the doctrine of the externality of relations, rooted in atomism and introducing associationism, can contribute to the critique of phenomenology or to the quest for the elemental world of Bergson are found in two enabling premises that Hume and Deleuze share. These are the principle of difference and the serialization/compossibility of different elements.[30] Empiricism, in Deleuze's reading of Hume, revolves around a principle of difference, holding that the given is a collection of ideas separable because different, and different because separable. This principle of difference requires that the mind be neither Subject nor Mirror of Nature. No impression is ever adventitious; all impressions are, in some sense, "innate."[31] Before the constitution of the Subject, no principle of organization rules over the mind. Only the indivisibility of impressions interests Hume, because it licenses his principle of difference and guarantees that the only constants of the mind will be indivisible atoms. It follows, argues Deleuze, that empiricism is not a philosophy of the senses but a philosophy of the imagination, and the statement that "all ideas are derived from impressions" is not meant to enshrine representationalism but is rather a regulative principle meant to keep us within the straight and narrow of the atomist principle of difference.

Of course, difference alone does not make an empiricist philosophy: difference *and* repetition are required to relate to each other chiastically.[32] From a host of differential perceptions, a subject is born inside the given, and the imagination is transformed into a faculty. Terms are related and serialized. When a law of reproduction of representations is formed under the impact of the principles of human nature, the subject comes to be, and begins to transcend the mind; it goes beyond the given. But repetition cannot occur without difference: the principles of human nature may well be the necessary condition for relations in general, serializations in general, or the advent of the structure-subject. However, particular relations and actual subjects require concrete and different circumstances as their sufficient conditions. Circumstances define passions and give direction to interests because affectivity and circumstance go together. And given the primacy assigned to the practical interest over the theoretical, the principles of passion are indispensable for the formation of concrete associations, and therefore indispensable for the constitution of the subject inside the mind.[33]

Ultimately, Deleuze's choice of empiricism amounts to a choice calculated to displace dialectics. The principle of difference that Deleuze locates in the heart of the Humean text prevents the closure threatened by dialectical sublation. Hypotactic subsumptions are replaced by paratactic conjunctions and arborite constructions give way to the strategy of the AND. Repetition—time and also habit as repetition—holds the paratactic series together, making possible their convergence and compossibility as well as their divergence and resonance. Difference and repetition displace the dialectical labor of the concept and thwart the mobilization of negation for the sake of allegedly superior synthesis.

The choice of empiricism is nothing less than a choice for a critical but nontranscendental philosophy. Transcendental philosophy, says Deleuze, beginning with a methodologically reduced field from which it derives essential certainty, asks how there can be a given, or how a subject can give itself the given. But Hume's empiricism asks how a subject can be constituted inside the given. The subject here is a task which must be fulfilled. In the process of fulfilling this task, empiricism generates a critique of rules by means of rules:

extensive rules are criticized and rectified through the application of corrective rules.[34] But to the extent that both kinds of rules find their origin in habit, the idea of an empiricist critique would be impossible and unintelligible were it not for the fact that habit is not solely the product of an experientially ascertained repetition of similar cases. Habit can be formed by other kinds of repetition as well. The task assumed by empiricism, therefore, is the constant correction of the imagination by means of the understanding. Habit extends the range of imagination but also corrects the accuracy of judgment. Critique must discipline the anticipating subject and make it focus on objects determined in accordance with the nature of the understanding and the weight of observed repetitions; critique must also educate the moral activity of the subject, that is, the act which accords with the intensive integration of disparate sympathies. But ultimately, Deleuze-Hume cannot prevent a paradox from being inscribed in the heart of empiricism: the same critique which disciplines the mind and prompts it to reject the fictions of the imagination is also the critique responsible for leading the mind to the biggest of all fictions—Subject, World, and God—and for turning these fictions into "incorrigible," constitutive ideas. In opposition to the prudential demarcation of ideas from concepts, which later on will be the pride of the Kantian critique, the Deleuzian-Humean empiricist critique will assign to the intensive idea the role of generating extensive concepts.[35] With Hume, the boldest moment of critical theory has come: the efficacy of the critique depends now on a fiction.

III

Avoir des raisons pour croire c'est d'avoir un corps. Le corps grec est une matière informée par une belle forme; il est le corps du savoir et de la croyance. Mais pour les modernes, il y a du temps dans le corps. Le nôtre c'est un corps tragile, toujours fatigué. Mettre dans le corps la fatigue, l'attente, c'est ça le corps qu'incorpore le temps.

—Gilles Deleuze, Paris VIII Seminar,
November 20, 1984

Many connoisseurs of the debates surrounding the lives and the deaths of the (neostructuralist!) subject have complained that the underdetermined or even indeterminate (not to be confused with "undecidable")[36] content of the notion "subjectivity" often leaves the debate without a point. The jury is still out, trying to nail down the precise moment of the subject's ingress in the "neostructuralist" body, and voices are raised for the reprieve of the praxiological subject or for the memorial repetition of the post-Messianic subject which is "never yet p."[37] But was it ever clear that the "neostructuralists"[38] had so unceremoniously ousted the subject from their discourse?

Strengthening the conviction that the ejection did occur is the posting, by friends and foes alike, of a composite picture of the neostructuralists which is everyone's and no one's. The montage which makes this composite picture possible verifies Bishop Berkeley's suspicion that behind every abstract generality one can always find the sharp outline of the features of one of the many family members. But then the problem with composite pictures is that they offer, on demand, some pretty convenient alibis: with their help, an examplaristic hermeneutics is brought to bear on a single family member, alleging at the same time that any other member of the family could have been an equally good choice; and while this is said, the artist is assured of a quick exit if his bluff is called. A composite picture, after all, must blur—if not obliterate—individual differences. I am not suggesting, of course, that there is something inherently vile in composite pictures; on the contrary, I am leading toward the suggestion that we must take them much more seriously than we have done. There is, after all, a neostructuralist *doxa*, presupposed and entailed by the labors of the neostructuralists we read. But this *doxa* is fissured and cracked; it envelops lines of flight and plateaus of (invented) compossibilities; and it brings together colliding forces along with the unstable consensus of a *concordia discordata*. Taking this *doxa* seriously presupposes a montage which operates on sharp-focused and skillfully developed singular frames. Lenses, made to adjust quickly between high and low altitudes, seem to be indispensable for carrying out this task.

It will be foolish, of course, to deny that the death of a certain subject has really been wished for, and that it has, perhaps, really happened. Rumor has it that the death has been wished for in the wake of a certain deadly violence perpetrated against the Other.[39] In this case, the resurrection of another Self and of an (otherwise) Other had understandably to wait for the completion of the critique of the Cartesian, Kantian, and Husserlian subject, and for the un-masking of the fraudulent accreditation that this subject had received in classical and modern texts. All this is well known; but what the composite picture of the neostructuralists renders invisible is the fact that not everyone who wished the death of "the" subject and the advent of a new entity in its place did share the same motivation for the wish or the same vision for the new dawn.

Deleuze undoubtedly is among those who contributed decisively to the critical unmasking of old pretensions and to the hopeful in-vigilation for the arrival of the new. An important "theory of sub-jectivity" runs through his entire work, beginning with the essay on Hume and reaching impressive depth and precision with his essay on Leibniz. What is remarkable, first of all, about this contribution to a theory of subjectivity is that it combines a radical critique of interiority with a stubborn search for "an inside that lies deeper than any internal world."[40] In this sense, the search for the *fold*—"the inside as the operation of the outside"[41]—that Deleuze so gallantly attributed to Foucault, is as much his own life-long search as it was (for a more limited time span) his friend's.

There is no doubt that Deleuze's theory is marked by the tension created by a radical critique of interiority and a simultaneous quest for an inside deeper than any internal world. But, as Manfred Frank (much more convincing in his studies of modern subjectivity than in his parody of neostructuralism) has shown, this tension is una-voidable in all theories of subjectivity mindful of the bankruptcy of models based on the classical optical metaphor, the egological field, and more generally every relational account of the structure con-sciousness/self-consciousness.[42] It is not strange, therefore, that De-leuze's contribution to the theory of subjectivity, mindful as it is of the opening up of a new space for a new Subject, after the bankruptcy of the old, experiences the same tension.

But whatever the advantages or the shortcomings of Deleuze's contribution may be, this contribution cannot be assessed fairly so long as the wrong strategies for reading Deleuze persist and con-tribute to the clouding of the issues. Deleuze's own rhizomatic growth and his strategy of writing should have warned against hom-ocentric evolutionist readings. In fact, any example of his writing on subjectivity taken from his texts would have sufficed to show that no reading of this kind had a chance to succeed. Consider, for example, the following three passages: (1) "The subject is defined by the movement through which it is developed." Believing and inventing is what makes the subject to be subject (*Empiricism and Subjectivity* [1953]);[43] (2) "There are no more subjects but dynamic individuation without subjects, which constitute collective assemblages. ... Nothing becomes subjective but hecceities take shape according to the compositions of non-subjective powers and effects" (*Dialogues* [1977]);[44] (3) "The struggle for [modern] subjectivity presents itself, therefore, as the right to difference, variation and metamorphosis" (*Foucault* [1986]).[45] How are these three statements to be shown compossible through the application of homocentric and evolutionist reading strategies?

It may seem, for a while, more promising to try and tease out of Deleuze's texts a theory of subjectivity after we adjust our interpretive lenses to the sort of periodization that a certain (questionable) reception of the "final Foucault" made fashionable. An arc would then run through Deleuze's writings, leading from an early historico-philosophical interest in the structure-Subject and its actualization (essay on Hume), through a middle period marked by the arrogant and suicidal pulverization of subjectivity (May 1968? Félix?), to a belated, timid retrieval of the Subject as folded interiority (*Foucault, Le Pli*).

The trouble with this periodization, however, is that it is too facile. It overlooks, once again, the rhizome named "Deleuze" and bypasses the complex relationships that exist between Deleuzian texts. *The Logic of Sense* (1969), for example, orchestrates the discussions on subjectivity around essays published and composed long before the chronological punctum of the explosion of desires. It cannot be read as a neostructuralist manifesto celebrating the pulverization of the Subject; it is too sober for that. Yet, this book anticipates and prepares *Capitalism and Schizophrenia* (1972, 1980), clearing up a transcendental field inhabited by singularities, events, or intensities and striated with lines converging for the creation of worlds, or with series of worlds diverging and resonant. A radical displacement of phenomenology is undoubtedly at work in this text, culminating in the "greening" of the philosophy of difference. But, on the other hand, this new focus does not prevent the series of *The Logic of Sense* from being consistent with the theses on subjectivity, already posted in the essay on Hume's theory of human nature. The structure of the Subject (belief and anticipation) *and also* the variable strategies for its actualization inside changing circumstances are themes common to them both. It would be fair to say that *The Logic of Sense* approaches the *Je et les dessous du Je*[46] in an entirely novel and fascinating way: its singularities and its converging or diverging lines are now full-fledged intensities, struggling to avoid thermic death in the course of being stretched and extended. But then again intensity does not make its appearance for the first time here: only a careless reading of Deleuze's earlier texts on Hume, on Nietzsche, and on Bergson can sidestep the theory of intensive time, already developed and pivotal in them.[47]

The only way, I think, to assess correctly Deleuze's contributions toward a theory of subjectivity is to read him the way he reads others: we must read him according to the series he creates, observing their ways of converging and of becoming compossible, or—and this amounts to the same thing for our strategy of reading—according to the series on their way to diverging and beginning to resonate. A relentless vigilance is necessary in every step of such a reading. It will be a mistake, for example, to take each book of Deleuze for one series, and to try to establish compossibility or resonance among the various books. I do not doubt that the names of those that Deleuze reads and writes about stand for singular points (intensities), capable of generating series. In this sense, one could, with justification, speak of a Hume-series, a Bergson-series, a Leibniz-series, etc. But none of these series is coextensive with the text or texts that bear the name of the thinker after whom a series has been named. Books and series do not coincide. This is why it would be better to talk about the "Hume-effect" series, the "Leibniz-effect" series, etc.

At any rate provided that we take adequate precautions, there is no harm in trying to spread Deleuze's contributions to a theory of subjectivity along the following series, each one of which could be identified by means of the question/problem introducing it. The *Hume-series* (how does the mind become a subject?); the *Bergson-series* (how can a static ontological genesis of the subject be worked out beginning with prepersonal and preindividual singularities and events?); the *Leibniz-series* (how can there be a notion of individuality which is neither a mere deduction from the concept "Subject"—in which case it would be contradictory—nor a mere figure of an individuality deprived of concept—in which case it would be absurd and ineffable?); the *Nietzsche-Foucault-series* (how can a dynamic genesis of subjectivity be constructed, in which the subject would be the folding and internalization of Outside forces, without succumbing to a philosophy of interiority?); the *Nietzsche-Klossowski-series* (how is it possible to think the subject in terms of inclusive disjunctions and simultaneously affirmed incompossible worlds?). These series would have run along their own lines of flight, without permitting the construction of any planes of consistency among them, were it not for Deleuze's concepts *"chaosmos"* = *chaos* + *cosmos* and "cracked I" *(Je fêlé)*, which in their capacity as portmanteau words circulate through the series and make possible the inclusive, disjunctive affirmation of all series. It is *chaosmos*, that is to say, the becoming-world, that posits the constitution of the subject as a task, and *chaosmos* again that guarantees that the constituted subject will not emerge as a substantive *hypokeimenon*, but rather as an already always "cracked I."

It is indeed striking to find the germs of all these series present in an early work like *Empiricism and Subjectivity*. *Empiricism and Subjectivity* is, for the most part, a segment of the Hume-series, without this fact preventing it from being also crisscrossed by segments of other series. It speaks of the structure—Subject in terms of anticipation and invention; it also introduces the actualization of the Subject in terms of concrete and always changing circumstances. It is coordinated by the question "how does the mind become subject?" and weaves the structure of subjectivity in terms of belief, anticipation and inventiveness. The Subject, in this series, is possible only as the correlate of the fictional idea "World." The constitutive function of the latter seals and makes possible the constitutive function of the principles of human nature.

Subjects anticipate and invent; in fact, they anticipate because they invent, and they invent always in concrete circumstances. The anticipatory and inventive subject will dot Deleuze's writings, without exception, although later, anticipation will be called by other names ("repetition," "absolute memory"), and invention will acquire its own synonyms ("assembling," "becoming on a line of flight," "becoming-other," etc.).[48] Deleuze will never waver in his conviction that only empiricists have the right access to the problem of subjectivity. Nonempiricists always endow their transcendental fields with individuality and personality, that is, with subjective Selfhood and personal Otherness, replicating thereby the empirical domain at the very moment that they allege to be in the process of grounding it. Empiricists, on the contrary, begin with the mind as a theater without a stage; they begin with the mind as delirium, contingency, and indifference and strive to understand how a mere collection of images can ever become a system. How can the mind become a subject? How can it become human nature? Deleuze-Hume's answer is that the mind becomes subject, that is, an entity capable of believing, anticipating, and inventing, as the result of the combined effects upon it of the principles of human nature. These principles, whether as principles of association or as principles of passion, pursue a selective and a corrective course: they select impressions of sensation, designate them as candidates for association, and, on this basis, they constitute impressions of reflection. In the case of cognition, the principles of association—contiguity, resemblance, and causality—designate impressions and organize the given into a system, bringing thereby constancy to the mind and naturalizing it. They form habit, they establish belief, and they constitute the subject as an entity that anticipates.

On the other hand, Deleuze recognizes that the constitution of the ethical subject presents Hume with a different problem: although the building blocks of morality are naturally given, they tend nonetheless to exclude one another. The mind experiences sympathy naturally. But our sympathies are partial, limited, and narrowly focused; if violence is to be avoided, the extension of our sympathies requires corrective integration.[49] Only through integration can the ethical totality be brought about, as an invention and an artifice. General rules, both extensive and corrective, must be invented and allowed to guide the operations of the principles of passion, for the sake of the integration of sympathies and for the constitution of the ethical subject.

For Deleuze-Hume, therefore, subjects affirm more than they know, and transcend their partiality in their moral acts; they believe, as this allows them to infer one (nongiven) part of nature from another which is already given; and they constitute ethical totalities by inventing institutions which nature does not provide. In both cases (knowledge and ethics), the subject transcends the given, albeit not in the same manner—at least not initially. Transcendence, in the case of knowledge, implies extending the Same or the Similar over parts which are external to one another, whereas transcendence, in the case of ethics, involves the intensity of the integrative act. The famous pair of categories, extension-intensity, around which the entire Deleuzian theory of difference and repetition will be orchestrated, has therefore found in the Humean empiricism an important ally and a vital inspiration: neither one will ever be abandoned.

But, as we now know from Deleuze's later work, the relations between the extension of contemplation and the intensity of practice are not as unproblematic and unidimensional as my last paragraph seems to suggest. Intensity and extension as world-making tendencies are not opposite poles in a field of exclusive disjunctions. An anticipation of their complex relationship in an early work such as *Empiricism and Subjectivity* is, in fact, striking. It centers on Deleuze's discussion of Humean time and on the function that time has in the constitution of subjectivity. Time was initially introduced by Hume as the structure of the mind; but the subject, formed by the habit inside the mind, is the synthesis of time. The mind was succession; the subject is now *durée* and anticipation. The anticipating and inventing subject constitutes the past which weighs on the present, making it pass, while positing the past as the rule for the future. Time as the constitutive force of subjectivity, responsible for the bending and folding of the given and the formation of interiority, is indeed intensive.

The same braiding of intensity and extension is discovered by Deleuze in the complex relations that Hume assigns to the principles of association and passion: passions require the association of ideas, but on the other hand the association of ideas presupposes passions.[50] The understanding reflects on our interest and socializes passion; but passions also give a disposition, an inclination, and a direction to the association. Ultimately, though, the relations between epistemic association and inclining passion are weighted in favor of the intensity of the passion, since there would be no association of ideas without the tendency-creating passions. Associations without passions are blind, but then passions without associations would be empty. The weight of this Humean move is not lost on Deleuze: it explains why no theory of subjectivity can be successful if it relies on the cognitive subject only. The problem can be correctly raised only at the level of practice, and the issues surrounding subjectivity cannot be dissociated from the imperatives of experimentation and struggle.

Moreover, the primacy of practice in the correct articulation of the structure-subjectivity resurfaces during Deleuze-Hume's discussion of the actualization of this structure in concrete subjects. The principles of association alone cannot account for the difference between subjects. Only concrete circumstances can explain the facts of differentiation. A differential psychology, as the science of the particular, must therefore reveal these circumstances. Deleuze will then reiterate Hume's position which asserts that subjectivity acquires its form through the principles of association while it is individuated through the principles of passion. Affectivity activates a tendency of the subject making her want to identify with the effects of her actions in all cases where these effects are the result of the means chosen. Once again, therefore, subjectivity is essentially linked with practice, for only a mind endowed with ends, and relations corresponding to these ends, can be a subject. Associationism is the theory of all that is practical, and operates only when harmony between fiction and the principles of passion has been established.

It should be obvious, despite the Humean tenor of the discussion, that the stakes are in fact about the practical and speculative interests of human subjects. The intensive, integrative act of the practical interest and its priority over the cognitive-speculative interest make possible the organization of subjectivity. But the peculiarity of the Hume-series is that it posits the subject as an always already "cracked subject." To disclose the cracks in the structure, Deleuze-Hume must direct his attention to the indispensable role that fiction plays in the structuration of the subject and to the constitution of individuality.

The subject, as we have seen, is the product of the principles of human nature; but then the mind, or the given, is the product of the powers of nature. Under these terms, the combined labor of passioned intensity and of the extensive use of associative principles would be spent in vain, as long as no firm relation has been established between the principles of human nature and the principles of nature.

Deleuze, therefore, in one of the most ingenious and most controversial gestures of the entire Hume-series, turns to Hume's discussions of religion, and fastens his analysis on the retrieval of purposiveness (*finalité*), made possible by these discussions, and its reentry into the world. Hume concedes that principles of association and passion (in both their extensive and their corrective function), jointly operate in the realm of religion. Deleuze then argues that, despite contrary textual appearances, Hume's corrective rules do not refute religion. On the contrary, theism is justified as soon as a certain antinomy affecting our ways of thinking about the world is resolved. On one hand, Hume is clear that the world is not an object; objects are in the world. It follows that the world cannot function in an argument, or be made to stand for an effect in a causal narrative, which would sing the glory of God's causal authorship. This stricture allows Hume to criticize teleological arguments and their God-founding pretensions. But there is something more in Hume, and Deleuze is not letting it go unnoticed. The world is always, for Hume, a fiction of the imagination; "but with the world, fiction becomes a horizon of experience, a principle of human nature which must co-exist with the other principles, despite the contradictions."[51] The world abides as a fiction of the imagination, *and also* fiction becomes a principle of human nature; the world never turns into an object of the understanding. It remains as an idea, but the idea is now constitutive; it constitutes a fiction.

Hume's empiricism, then, in Deleuze's estimate, shows the subject in the process of being constituted on a soil already eroded by a contradiction without possible conciliation. In the antinomy of the world, the imagination with its fiction is opposed to the principles which fix it and the operations which correct it. Under these circumstances, extension and reflection find themselves on a collision course: an opposition reigns supreme between the principles of association and the fiction which has become a principle of nature. No choice is possible between the understanding and the suggestions of the imagination: for "when fiction becomes principle, reflection does not stop reflecting, nonetheless it can no longer correct."[52] All the systematization, naturalization, and subjectivation of the mind that we witnessed so far have not helped the mind silence its delirium.

Yet it is the same delirium that makes possible the solution of the antinomy of the world. Hume, according to Deleuze, prohibits the mobilization of the principles of human nature for the sake of proving that the world is God's effect; the same Hume, though, is not opposed to thinking of God negatively, as the cause of these principles. This decision, concludes Deleuze, reestablishes purposiveness to the extent that it makes the agreement between the principles of human nature and the hidden powers of nature *thinkable* again.[53] A long quotation from Deleuze's chapter on Hume in *La Philosophie* forcefully makes this point: it characterizes the stages by means of which the real world becomes a fiction before the opposition of reality and fiction is overcome.

> In opposition to ancient scepticism which rests on the variability of sensible appearance and on the errors of the senses, modern scepticism rests on the status of relations and on their exteriority. The first act of modern scepticism was the discovery of belief in the foundations of knowledge, that is, the naturalization of belief (positivism). Starting from this point, its second act was the denunciation of illegitimate beliefs, that is, of beliefs which do not obey the rules which result in effective knowledge (probabilism, calculus of probabilities). However, in a last refinement and in a third act, *the illegitimate beliefs in the World, the Self and God appear as the horizon of all possible legitimate beliefs, or as the lowest degree of belief.*[54] [The italics are mine.]

Incipit simulacrum!

ONE

THE PROBLEM OF
KNOWLEDGE
AND THE PROBLEM
OF ETHICS

HUME PROPOSES THE creation of a science of humanity, but what is really his fundamental project? A choice is always defined in terms of what it excludes, and a historical project is a logical substitution. Hume's project entails the *substitution of a psychology of the mind by a psychology of the mind's affections*. The constitution of a psychology of the mind is not at all possible, since this psychology cannot find in its object the required constancy or universality; only a psychology of affections will be capable of constituting the true science of humanity.

In this sense, Hume is a moralist and a sociologist, before being a psychologist; the *Treatise* shows that the two forms under which the mind is *affected* are essentially the *passional* and the *social*. They imply each other, assuring thereby the unity of the object of an authentic science. On one hand, society demands and expects from each one of its members the display of constant reactions, the presence of passions able to provide motives and ends, and the availability of collective or individual characters: "A prince, who imposes a tax upon his subjects, expects their compliance."[1] On the other hand, the passions implicate society as the oblique means for their satisfaction.[2] In the last analysis, the coherence of the passional and the social, in history, is revealed as an internal unity, with political organization and the institutions giving history its objects. History studies the relations between motive and action in most circumstances, and it also exhibits the uniformity of the human passions. In brief, the option of the psychologist may be expressed paradoxically as follows: one must be a moralist, sociologist, or historian *before* being a psychologist, *in order to* be a psychologist. Here, the project of the human sciences reaches the condition which would make knowledge in general possible: the mind must be affected. By itself and in itself, the mind is not nature; it is not the object of science. Hence, the question which will preoccupy Hume is this: *how does the mind become human nature?*

Passional *and* social affection are only a part of human nature; there are also the understanding and the association of ideas. The fact is, though, that this list is still based on convention. The real role of the understanding, says Hume, is to make the passions sociable and the interest social. The understanding reflects interest. *On the other hand,* nothing prevents us from thinking of it as something distinct, the way the physicist fragments a movement, while recognizing all along that it is indivisible and noncomposite.[3] We should not, in fact, forget that two points of view coexist in Hume: the passions and the understanding present themselves, in a way which must be made clear, as two distinct parts. By itself, though, the understanding is only the process of the passions on their way to socialization. Sometimes we see that the understanding and the passions constitute two separate problems, but at other times, we see that the understanding is subordinated to the passions. This is the reason why, even when studied separately, the understanding must above all help us to understand better the general sense of the above question.

Hume constantly affirms the identity between the mind, the imagination, and ideas. The mind is not nature, nor does it have a nature. It is identical with the ideas in the mind. Ideas are given, as given; they are experience. The mind, on the other hand, is given as a collection of ideas and not as a system. It follows that our earlier question can be expressed as follows: how does a collection become a system? The collection of ideas is called "imagination," insofar as the collection designates not a faculty but rather an assemblage of things, in the most vague sense of the term: things are as they appear—a collection without an album, a play without a stage, a flux of perceptions. "The comparison of the theatre must not mislead us; nor have we the most distant notion of the place, where these scenes are represented, or of the materials, of which it is compos'd."[4] The place is not different from what takes place in it; the representation does not take place in a subject. Then again the question may be: *how does the mind become a subject*? How does the imagination become a faculty?

It is true, Hume constantly reiterates, that ideas are *in* the imagination. But the preposition here does not signify inherence in a subject; rather, the use of the preposition is metaphorical, and it means to exclude from the mind an activity which would be distinct from the movement of ideas; it means to ensure the identity between the mind and the ideas in the mind. The preposition signifies that the imagination is not a factor, an agent, or a determining determination. It is a place which must be localized, that is to say, fixed—something determinable. Nothing is done *by* the imagination; everything is done *in* the imagination. It is not even a faculty for forming ideas, because the production of an idea by the imagination is only the reproduction of an impression in the imagination. Certainly, the imagination has its own activity; but even this activity, being whimsical and delirious, is without constancy and without uniformity. It is the movement of ideas, and the totality of their actions and reactions. Being the place of ideas, the fancy is the collection of separate, individual items. Being the bond of ideas, it moves through the universe,[5] engendering fire dragons, winged horses, and monstrous giants.[6] The depth of the mind is indeed delirium, or—same thing from another point of view—change and indifference.[7] By itself, the imagination is not nature; it is a mere fancy. There is no constancy or uniformity in the ideas that I have. No more is there constancy or uniformity in the way *in which ideas are connected through the imagination:* only chance makes up this connection.[8] The generality of the idea is not a characteristic of the idea; it does not belong to the imagination: rather than being the nature of some idea, it is a *role* which every idea can play under the influence of other principles.

What are these other principles? How does the imagination become human nature? Constancy and uniformity are present only in the way *in which ideas are associated in the imagination.* Association, with its three principles (contiguity, resemblance, and causality), transcends the imagination, and also differs from it. Association affects the imagination. Rather than finding its origin, association finds in the imagination its term and its object. It is a quality which unifies ideas, not a quality of ideas themselves.[9]

As we will see, through belief and causality the subject *transcends* the given. Literally, the subject goes beyond what the mind gives it: I believe in what I have neither seen nor touched. But the subject can go beyond the given because *first of all* it is, *inside the mind*, the effect of principles transcending and affecting the mind. Before there can be belief, all three principles of association must organize the given into a system, imposing constancy on the imagination. The latter does not draw its own resources from constancy, but without it, it would never be a human nature. These principles attribute to ideas the links and principles of union, which, instead of being the characteristics of ideas, are the original qualities of human nature.[10] The privilege that causality enjoys is that it alone can make us affirm existence and make us believe. It confers upon the idea of the object a solidity and an objectivity that this idea would not have had it only been associated through contiguity or resemblance to an actual impression.[11] But the other two principles also share with causality a common role: they fix and naturalize the mind; they prepare belief and accompany it. We can now see the special ground of empiricism: nothing in the mind transcends human nature, because it is human nature that, in its principles, transcends the mind; nothing is ever transcendental. Association, far from being a product, is a rule of the imagination and a manifestation of its free exercise. It guides the imagination, gives it uniformity, and also constrains it.[12] In this sense, ideas are connected in the mind—not by the mind.[13] The imagination is indeed human nature but only to the extent that other principles have made it constant and settled.

There is a difficulty, though, even with this definition. Why is regulated imagination, rather than the rule grasped in its active power, human nature? How can we say of the imagination that it *becomes* a nature, despite the fact that it has not within itself a reason for this becoming? The answer is simple. Essentially, principles refer to the mind which they affect, but nature refers to the imagination; its entire function is to qualify the imagination. Association is a law of nature, and like every other law, it is defined by its effects, not by a cause. Similarly, on an entirely different plane, God may be called "cause" and preestablished harmony or teleology may be fruitfully invoked.[14] The conclusion of the *Dialogues,* the essay on miracles, and the essay on immortality are in fact coherent. A cause may always be *thought,* as something in itself, transcending all the analogies which provide it with a determined content, in the case of experience and knowledge.[15] But the fact is that philosophy, being a human science, need not search for the cause; it should rather scrutinize effects. The cause cannot be *known;* principles have neither cause nor an origin of their power. What is original is their effect upon the imagination.

The effect of association appears in three ways.[16] Sometimes the idea takes on a role and becomes capable of representing all these ideas with which, through resemblance, it is associated (general idea); at other times, the union of ideas brought about *by* the mind acquires a regularity not previously had, in which case "nature in a manner point[s] out to every one those simple ideas, which are most proper to be united into a complex one"[17] (substance and mode); finally, sometimes, one idea can introduce another[18] (relation). The result of the association in all three cases is the mind's easy passage from one idea to another, so that the essence of relations becomes precisely this easy transition.[19] The mind, having become nature, has acquired now a *tendency*.

But despite the fact that nature makes reference to ideas, to the extent that it associates them in the mind, the ideas do not acquire a new quality of their own, nor are they capable of attributing it to their objects; no new ideas ever appear. Ideas are related in a uniform way, but those relations are not the object of an idea. Hume, in fact, observes that general ideas must be represented, but only in the *fancy,* under the form of a particular idea having a determined quantity and quality.[20] *On one hand,* the imagination cannot become in itself nature without being for itself the fancy. As for the fancy, it finds here an entirely new extension. The fancy can always invoke relations, borrow the clothing of nature, and form general rules, going beyond the determined field of legitimate knowledge and carrying knowledge beyond its proper limits. It can display *its own* fancies: the Irish cannot be witty, the French cannot have solidity.[21] In order to wipe out the effect of these extensive rules and in order to consolidate knowledge, we will need the application of different rules—

this time, the application of corrective rules. Albeit less fancifully, the imagination, whenever faced with a relation, will not fail to double and reinforce it by means of other relations, however unmerited they may be.[22]

On the other hand, the mind cannot be activated by the principles of nature without remaining passive. It only suffers the effects. Relations are not doing the connecting, but rather they themselves are connected; causality, for example, is passion, an impression of reflection,[23] and a "resemblance effect."[24] Causality is *felt*.[25] It is a perception of the mind and not a conclusion of the understanding: "We must not here be content with saying, that the idea of cause and effect arises from objects constantly united; but must affirm that 'tis the very same with the idea of these objects."[26] In short, the necessary relation is indeed in the subject, *but only insofar as the subject contemplates*.[27] This is the reason why Hume sometimes, on the negative side, insists on the paradox of his thesis; and at other times, on the positive side, he emphasizes its orthodoxy. Insofar as necessity is on the side of the subject, the necessary relation, in the case of things, is only a constant conjunction—*necessity is indeed only that*.[28] But necessity belongs to the subject only insofar as the subject contemplates, and not insofar as it acts.[29] The constant conjunction is *the entire* necessary relation.[30] For Hume, the determination is not determining; it is rather determined. When Hume speaks of an act of the mind—of a disposition—he does not mean to say that the mind is active but that it is activated and that it has become subject. The coherent paradox of Hume's philosophy is that it offers a subjectivity which transcends itself, without being any less passive. Subjectivity is determined as an effect; it is in fact an *impression of reflection*. The mind, having been affected by the principles, turns now into a subject.

Nature cannot be studied scientifically except in terms of its effects upon the mind, yet the only true science of the mind should have nature as its object. "Human Nature is the only science of man."[31] This, of course, means that the psychology of affections disallows any psychology of the mind, but it also means that affections give the mind its qualities. A certain ambiguity may well be explained in this way. In Hume's work, we witness the unequal development of two lines of diverse inspiration. On one hand, the psychology of the mind is a psychology of ideas, of simple elements, of minima or indivisibles. It occupies essentially the second part of the system of the understanding—"the ideas of space and time." This is Hume's *atomism*. On the other hand, the psychology of human nature is a psychology of dispositions, perhaps even an anthropology, a science of practice, especially morality, politics, and history. It is finally a real critique of psychology, insofar as it locates the reality of its object in all the determinations not given in an idea, or in all the qualities transcending the mind. This second line of inspiration constitutes Hume's *associationism*, and to confuse associationism with atomism is a curious misunderstanding.

Now, we are faced with the question: why does the first inspiration subsist in Hume's writings, especially in his theory of space? We have seen that, although the psychology of affections contains in its project the critique and even the elimination of a psychology of the mind (as a science impossible to constitute), it nevertheless contains in its object an essential reference to the mind as the objective of natural qualifications. Since the mind is in itself a collection of atoms, a true psychology is neither immediately nor directly possible: the principles do not make the mind an object of possible science without first giving it an objective nature. Hume therefore does not create an atomistic psychology; he rather indicates, inside atomism, a state of the mind which does not permit any psychology. We cannot reproach Hume for having neglected the important problem of the conditions of the human sciences. We might even wonder whether modern authors do not repeat Hume's philosophical project when they associate an assiduous critique of atomism with every positive moment of the human sciences. It would follow that they treat atomism less as a historical localized thesis and more as the general schema of what psychology cannot be; they condemn it, therefore, in the name of the concrete rights of ethology and sociology, or of the passional and the social.

> "The intellect," said Comte with respect to impossible psychologies, "is almost exclusively the subject of their speculations, and the affections have been almost entirely neglected; and, moreover, always subordinated to the understanding. . . . The whole of *human nature* is thus very unfaithfully represented by these futile systems. . . ."[32]

All serious writers agree on the impossibility of a psychology of the mind. This is why they criticize so meticulously every single identification between consciousness and knowledge. They differ only in the way they determine the factors which give a nature to the mind. Sometimes, these factors are the body and matter, in which case psychology makes room for physiology. Sometimes they are particular principles, constituting a psychic equivalent of matter, wherein psychology finds its unique, possible object and its scientific condition. Hume, with his principles of association, has chosen the latter route, which is the most difficult and the most audacious. This is where his sympathy for materialism comes from, and at the same time his reticence toward it.

Until now, we have shown only that the task that Hume's philosophy sets for itself is to answer the question "how does the mind become a nature." But *why* is it this one? The question must be taken up on a different plane. Hume's problem would then be exclusively about a fact, and therefore empirical. *Quid facti?* What is the fact of knowledge? It is transcendence or going beyond. I affirm more than I know; my judgment goes beyond the idea. In other words, *I am a subject.* I say "Caesar is dead," "the sun will rise tomorrow," "Rome exists"; I speak in general terms and I have beliefs, I establish relations—this is a fact and a practice. In the case of knowledge, where is the fact? *The fact is* that these practices cannot be expressed in the form of an idea without the idea becoming immediately contradictory. Take, for example, the incompatibility between a general or abstract idea and the nature of an idea,[33] or between a real relation between objects and the objects to which we apply the relation.[34] The more immediate or immediately decided the incompatibility is, the more decisive it will be.[35] Hume does not reach this point after a long discussion, *he begins with it,* so that the point about the contradiction assumes naturally the role of a basic challenge. This is the only relation between the philosopher and the others inside the system of the understanding.[36] "Show me the idea you claim to have." What's at stake in the challenge is the very psychology of mind. In fact, the given and experience have now two inverse meanings. The given is the idea as it is given in the mind, without anything transcending it—not even the mind, which is therefore identical with the idea. But, the transcendence itself is also given, in an altogether different sense and manner—it is given as practice, as an affection of the mind, and as an impression of reflection: passion, says Hume, does not have to be defined:[37] by the same token, belief is a *je ne sais quoi* adequately felt by everyone.[38] Empirical subjectivity is constituted in the mind under the influence of principles affecting it; the mind therefore does not have the characteristics of a preexisting subject. True psychology, that is, the psychology of affections, will be duplicated in each one of its moments by means of a critique of the false psychology of the mind; the latter is in fact incapable of grasping without contradiction the constitutive element of human reality. But why *is it finally necessary* that philosophy undertake this critique, express the transcendence in an idea, produce the contradiction, and manifest the incompatibility as the fact of knowledge?

It is because the transcendence under discussion is not given in an idea, but is rather referred to the mind; it qualifies the mind. The mind is at the same time the object of a critique and the term of a necessary reference. The necessity of the critique is located here. This is the reason why, with respect to questions of the understanding, Hume's method is always the same: it goes from the absence of an idea in the mind to the presence of an affection of the mind. The negation of the idea of a thing affirms the identity between the character of this thing and the nature of an impression of reflection. This is the case with existence, general ideas, necessary connection, the self, and also vice and virtue. In all these cases, instead of negating the criterion of the idea, we allow the negation of the idea itself to serve as a criterion; transcendence is first and foremost understood in its negative relation to that which it transcends.[39] Conversely, in the structures of transcendence, the mind finds a kind of positivity which comes to it from outside.

But then, how can we reconcile this entire method with Hume's principle, according to which all ideas derive from a corresponding impression and, consequently, *every* given impression is reproduced in an idea which perfectly represents it? If, for example, necessity is an impression of reflection, there must necessarily be an idea of necessity.[40] Critique, says Hume, does not deprive the idea of necessary connection of its sense, it only destroys its improper applications.[41] There certainly is an idea of necessity. But basically, we speak of an impression of reflection, whenever the necessary relation is the mind affected and determined (in certain circumstances) by the idea of an object to form the idea of another object. The impression of necessity, because it is a qualification of the mind, would not be able to produce the idea as a quality of things. The proper role of the impressions of reflection, being effects of the principles, is to *qualify* in various ways the mind as subject. Affections then unveil the idea of subjectivity. *The term "idea" can no longer have the same meaning.* Consequently, the psychology of affections becomes the philosophy of the constituted subject.

Rationalism has lost this philosophy. Hume's philosophy is a sharp critique of representation. It does not elaborate a critique of relations but rather a critique of representations, precisely because representations *cannot* present relations. By making representation into a criterion and by placing ideas within reason, rationalism expects ideas to stand for something which cannot be constituted within experience or be given in an idea without contradiction: the generality of the idea, the existence of the object, and the content of the terms "always," "universal," "necessary," and "true." Rationalism has transferred mental determinations to external objects, taking away thereby from philosophy the meaning and the intelligibility of practice and of the subject. The fact is, though, that the mind is not reason; reason is an affection of the mind. In this sense, reason will be called instinct,[42] habit, or nature.[43] "[W]e have found [reason] to be nothing but a general calm determination of the passions, founded on some distant view or reflexion."[44]

Reason is a kind of feeling. Consequently, just as the method of philosophy goes from the absence of an idea to the presence of an impression, similarly the theory of reason moves also from a kind of skepticism to a kind of positivism. It moves from a skepticism of reason to a positivism of feeling, in which case the latter includes reason as a reflection of feeling in the qualified mind.

In the same way that a distinction is made between atomism and associationism, a distinction must also be made between the two senses of the term "idea," and therefore the two senses of the term "impression." In one sense, we do not have the idea of necessity, but in another, we do. Despite the texts which present simultaneously and render homogeneous as much as possible[45] the impressions of sensation and the impressions of reflection (or the ideas of sensation and the ideas of reflection), the difference between the two is really a difference of nature. Witness, for example, the following quotation:

> For *that* is necessary to produce a new idea of reflection, nor
> can the mind, by revolving over a thousand times all its ideas
> of sensation, ever extract from them any new original idea,
> *unless nature has so fram'd its faculties,* that it feels some new
> original impression arise from such a contemplation.[46]

The impressions of sensation are only the origin of the mind; as
for the impressions of reflection, they are the qualification of the
mind and the effect of principles in it. The point of view of the
origin, according to which every idea derives from a preexisting
impression and represents it, does not have the importance that people attribute to it: it merely gives the mind a simple origin and frees
the ideas from the obligation of having to represent *things,* and also
from the corresponding difficulty of having to understand the resemblance of ideas. The real importance is on the side of the impressions of reflection, because they are the ones which qualify the mind
as subject. The essence and the destiny of empiricism are not tied
to the atom but rather to the essence of association; therefore, empiricism does not raise the problem of the origin of the mind but
rather the problem of the constitution of the subject. Moreover, it
envisages this constitution in the mind as the effect of transcending
principles and not as the product of a genesis. The difficulty is in
establishing a specific relation between the two meanings of "idea"
or "impression," or between origin and qualification. We have already seen their difference. It is the same difference that Hume
encounters under the form of an antimony of knowledge: it defines
the problem of the self. The mind is not subject; it is subjected.
When the subject is constituted in the mind under the effect of
principles, the mind apprehends itself as a self, for it has been qualified. But the problem is this: if the subject is constituted only inside
the collection of ideas, how can the collection of ideas be apprehended as a self, how can I say "I," under the influence of those
same principles? We do not really understand how we can move
from dispositions to the self, or from the subject to the self. How
can the subject and the mind, in the last analysis, be one and the
same inside the self? The self must be both a collection of ideas and
a disposition, mind and subject. It is a synthesis, which is incom-
prehensible, since it ties together in its notion, without ever recon-
ciling them, origin and qualification.

> In short there are two principles, which I cannot render
> consistent; nor is it in my powers to renounce either of them,
> viz. *that all our distinct perceptions are distinct existences*, and
> *that the mind never perceives any real connexion among distinct
> existences*.[47]

Hume in fact adds that a solution may be possible. We will see later
on what sense we can give to this hope.

Human nature is the real object of science. But Hume's philosophy
presents us with two modalities of this nature and with two types
of affection: we are faced, on one hand, with the effects of association,
and on the other with the effects of passion. Each one of them
determines a system: the system of understanding and the system of
passions and ethics. But what is their relation? To begin with, between the two, a kind of parallelism seems to be established and
followed exactly. Belief and sympathy correspond. Moreover, everything that belongs to sympathy and goes beyond belief is, according
to the analysis, analogous to that which the passions add to the
association of ideas.[48] On another plane, just as association fixes in
the mind a necessary generality, that is, a rule which is indispensable
to theoretical knowledge, in the same way the passions provide the
mind with the content of a constancy,[49] make possible a practical
and moral activity, and give history its meaning. Without this double
movement, there would not even be a human nature, for the imagination would be mere fancy. The points of correspondence do not
stop there: the relation between motive and action is of a piece with
causality,[50] to the point that history must be construed as a physics
of humanity.[51] Finally, in the case of the determination of nature,
and in the case of the constitution of a world of morality, general
rules, being both extensive and corrective, have the same sense. We
should not identify the system of understanding with theory, and
the system of morality and the passions with practice. Under the
name of belief, we have a practice of the understanding, and under
the form of social organization and justice, a theory of morality.
Moreover, everywhere in Hume, the only possible theory is a theory
of practice: with respect to the understanding, we have the calculation of probabilities and general rules; with respect to morality and
the passions, we have general rules and justice.

Important as they may be, however, all these correspondences are the mere presentation of philosophy and the distribution of its results. The relation of analogy between the two constituted domains should not make us forget which one of them determines the constitution of the other as a philosophical matter. We actually seek the *motive* of philosophy. At least, the fact is easy to decide: Hume is above all a moralist, a political thinker, and a historian. But why?

The *Treatise* begins with the system of understanding, and raises the problem of reason. However, the necessity of such a problem is not obvious; it must have an origin, which we can consider as a motive of this philosophy. It is not because reason solves problems that it is itself a problem. On the contrary, for reason to experience a problem, in its own domain, there must be a domain that escapes reason, putting it initially into question. The important and principal sentence of the *Treatise* is this: " 'Tis not contrary to Reason to prefer the destruction of the whole world to the scratching of my finger."[52]

Contrariety is an excessive relation. Reason can be put into question and can raise the problem of its nature, because it does not apply to all there is. The fact is that it does not determine practice: it is practically or technically insufficient. Undoubtedly, reason influences practice, to the extent that it informs us of the existence of a thing, as the proper object of a passion, or to the extent that it reveals a connection between causes and effects as means of satisfaction.[53] But we cannot say that reason produces an action, that passion contradicts it, or even that reason thwarts a passion. Contradiction implies at least a disagreement between ideas and the objects which the ideas represent: "A passion is an original existence, or, if you will, modification of existence, and contains not any representative quality, which renders it a copy of any other existence or modification."[54]

Moreover, moral distinctions do not let themselves be engendered through reason; they arouse passions, and produce or hinder action.[55] There is indeed contradiction in misappropriating properties and in violating promises, but only to the extent that promises and properties exist in nature. Reason can always be brought to bear, but it is brought to bear on a preexisting world and presupposes an antecedent ethics and an order of ends.[56] Thus, it is because practice and morality are in their nature (and not in their circumstances) indifferent to reason that reason seeks its difference. Because it is negated from the outside, it is denied from the inside and discovered as madness and skepticism. Furthermore, because this skepticism has its origin and its motive on the outside, in the indifference of practice, practice itself is indifferent to skepticism: we can always play backgammon.[57] The philosopher behaves as anyone else: the characteristic of the skeptic is that her or his reasoning does not allow a reply and, at the same time, does not produce conviction.[58] We are, therefore, brought back to the previous conclusion, and this time we find it completed: skepticism and positivism are mutually implied by the same philosophical reasoning. The positivism of the passions and ethics produces a skepticism of reason. This internalized skepticism, having become a skepticism of reason, causes a positivism of the understanding as the theory of a practice. This positivism of the understanding is conceived in the image of the skepticism of reason.[59] According to the image, yes, but not according to the resemblance. We can now understand exactly the difference between the system of ethics and the system of the understanding. In the case of the affect, we must distinguish two terms: passional or moral affection, and transcendence as a dimension of knowledge. Without a doubt, the principles of morality, that is, the original and natural qualities of the passions, transcend and affect the mind, just as the principles of association do. The empirical subject is firmly constituted in the mind by the combined effect of all principles. But it is only under the (unequal) influence of the principles of association—not of the others—that this subject can transcend the given: it believes. In this precise sense, transcendence is exclusively the affair of knowledge: it carries the idea beyond itself, giving it a role, affirming its object, and constituting its links. It follows that in the system of the understanding, the most important principle which affects the mind will *first of all* be studied in activity, that is, in the movement of a subject that transcends the given: the nature of the causal relation is grasped in the context of the *inference*.[60] But the case of ethics is completely different, even when it takes analogically the form of the exposition of transcendence.[61] There is no inference to be drawn in this case. "We do not infer a character to be virtuous, because it pleases: But in feeling that it pleases after such a particular manner, we in effect feel that it is virtuous."[62] Ethics admits the idea as a factor only of the relevant circumstances and accepts the association as a constituted element of human nature. In the system of the understanding, on the other hand, association is a constitutive element—in fact, the only constitutive element of human nature. As an illustration of this duality, it is enough to remember Hume's distinction between two selves,[63] and the different way in which he presents and handles the corresponding problems.

Thus, there are two kinds of practice which are immediately marked by very distinctive characteristics. The practice of the understanding determines the internal economy of nature, and proceeds by means of extension. Nature, the object of physics, is *partes extra partes*. This is its essence. If we consider objects from the point of view of their idea, it is possible for all objects "to become causes or effects of each other,"[64] since the causal relation is not one of their qualities: from a logical point of view, anything could be the cause of anything. But if, on the other hand, we observe the conjunction of two objects, each of the numerically different cases which presents the conjunction is independent of the other; neither has influence over the other; "they are entirely divided by time and place."[65] They are only the component parts of a certain probability.[66] In fact, if probability presupposes causality, the certainty which is born of causal reasoning is also a limit and a particular case of probability, or rather the practically absolute convergence of probabilities.[67] Nature is indeed an extensive magnitude, and as such it lends itself to physical experiment and measurement. The essential thing is to determine the parts, and, within the realm of knowledge, this is the function of general rules. Nature is not a whole; the whole can no more be discovered than it can be invented. Totality is just a collection. ". . . I answer that the uniting of these parts into a whole, . . . is performed merely by an arbitrary act of the mind, and has no influence on the nature of things."[68] The general rules of knowledge, insofar as their generality concerns the whole, are not different from the natural principles of our understanding.[69] The difficulty, says Hume, is not in inventing but rather in applying them.

The case of the practice of morality, however, is different. Here, the parts are given immediately, without any inference required, and without any necessary application. But, *instead of being extensive, these parts are mutually exclusive;* they are not made up of parts *(partielles),* as in the case of nature; they are rather partial *(partiales).* In the ethical practice, the difficulty is in diverting and slanting that partiality. The important thing here is to invent: justice is an artificial virtue, and "man is an inventive species."[70] The essential task is to constitute a whole of morality; for justice is a *schema*,[71] and the schema is the very principle of society. "[A] single act of justice, consider'd in itself, may often be contrary to the public good; and 'tis only the concurrence of mankind, in a general scheme or system of action, which is advantageous."[72]

The question is no longer about transcendence but rather about integration. Unlike reason, which always proceeds from one part to another, feeling reacts to wholes.[73] This is why, in the domain of ethics, general rules have a different meaning.

TWO

CULTURAL WORLD
AND GENERAL RULES

WE MUST NOW explain some issues pertaining to ethics. It is the essence of moral conscience to approve and disapprove. The feeling which prompts us to praise or blame, the pain and pleasure which determine vice and virtue, have an original nature: they are produced with reference to character *in general,* and with no reference to our particular interest.[1] But what can make us abandon the reference to our own point of view, and make us refer, "through mere inspection," to character in general? In other words, what can make us take hold of something and live in it, because it is useful or agreeable to the Other or to persons in general? Hume's response is simple: sympathy. There is, however, a paradox of sympathy: it opens up for us a moral space and generality, but the space has no extension, nor does the generality have quantity. In fact, in order to be moral, sympathy must extend into the future and must not be limited to the present moment. It must be a *double* sympathy, that is, a correspondence of impressions multiplied by the desire for the pleasure of the Other and by an aversion for her or his pain.[2] It is a fact that sympathy exists and that it is extended naturally. But this extension is not affirmed without cultural exclusion: it is impossible for sympathy to extend "without being aided by some circumstance in the present, which strikes upon us in a lively manner,"[3] excluding thereby all cases which do not present these circumstances. The circumstances, from the point of view of the fancy, will be the degree or more precisely the enormity of unhappiness;[4] but from the point of view of human nature, there will be contiguity, resemblance, or causality. Those whom we love, according to circumstances, are those close to us, our peers and our relatives.[5] Briefly, our natural generosity is limited; what is natural to us is a limited generosity.[6] Sympathy extends itself naturally into the future, but only when the circumstances limit its extension. The other side of generality to which sympathy invites us is partiality, that is, an "inequality of affection" that sympathy bestows upon us as a characteristic of our nature, "so as to make us regard any remarkable transgression of such a degree of partiality, either by too great an enlargement, or contraction of the affections, as vicious and immoral."[7] We condemn the parents who prefer strangers to their own children.

Thus, it is not our nature which is moral, it is rather our morality which is in our nature. One of Hume's simplest but most important ideas is this: human beings are much less egoistic than they are *partial*. Some believe themselves to be philosophers and good thinkers, as they maintain that egoism is the last resort of every activity, but this is too simple. Do they not see that "there are few that do not bestow the largest part of their fortunes on the pleasures of their wives, and the education of their children, reserving the smallest portion for their own proper use and entertainment[?]"[8]

The truth is that an individual always belongs to a clan or a community. Before being the types of community that Tönnies described, family, friendship, and neighborliness are, in Hume's work, the natural determinants of sympathy. It is precisely because the essence of passion or the essence of the particular interest is partiality rather than egoism that sympathy, for its part, does not transcend the particular interest or passion. "Our sense of duty always follows the common and natural course of our passions."[9] Let us follow the argument through, even if we jeopardize the advantage of our distinction between egoism and sympathy: sympathy is no less opposed to society than egoism is. ". . . [S]o noble an affection, instead of fitting men for large societies, is almost as contrary to them, as the most narrow selfishness."[10]

No one has the same sympathies as another; given the plurality of partialities, we are confronted with contradiction and violence.[11]

This is nature's course; there is no reasonable human language at this level.

> ... [E]very particular man has a peculiar position with regard to others; and 'tis impossible we cou'd ever converse together on any reasonable terms, were each of us to consider characters and persons, only as they appear from his peculiar point of view.[12]

However, if sympathy is *like* egoism, what importance should we accord to Hume's observation that we are not egoistically but rather sympathetically inclined? The truth of the matter is that, even if society finds *as much* of an obstacle in sympathy as in the purest egoism, what changes absolutely is the sense or the structure of society itself, depending on whether we consider it from the point of view of egoism or sympathy. Egoisms would only have to be limited, but sympathies are another matter, for they must be integrated inside a positive totality. What Hume criticizes in contractarian theories is precisely that they present us with an abstract and false image of society, that they define society only in a negative way; they see in it a set of limitations of egoisms and interests instead of understanding society as a positive system of invented endeavors. That is why it is so important to be reminded that the natural human being is not egoist; our entire notion of society depends on it. What we find in nature, without exception, are families; the state of nature is always already more than a simple state of nature.[13] The family, independently of all legislation, is explained by the sexual instinct and by sympathy—sympathy between parents, and sympathy of parents for their offspring.[14] We should rather understand the problem of society from this angle, because society finds its obstacle in sympathies rather than in egoism. Without a doubt, society is in the beginning a collection of families; but a collection of families is not a family reunion. Of course, families are social units; but the characteristic of these units is that they are not added to one another. Rather, they exclude one another; they are partial (*partiales*) rather than made up of parts (*partielles*). The parents of one family are always the strangers of other families. Consequently, a contradiction explodes inside nature. The problem of society, in this sense, is not a problem of limitation, but rather a problem of integration. To integrate sympathies is to make sympathy transcend its contradiction and natural partiality. Such an integration implies a positive moral world, and is brought about by the positive invention of such a world.

It follows that the moral world is not reduced to a moral instinct or to the natural determinations of sympathy.[15] The moral world affirms its reality when the contradiction is effectively dissipated, when conversation is possible as an alternative to violence, when property supersedes greed, when "notwithstanding this variation of our sympathy, we give the same approbation to the same moral qualities in *China* as in *England*," or, in a word, when "the sympathy varies without a variation in our esteem."[16]

Esteem is the factor which integrates sympathies, and the foundation of justice. This foundation or this uniformity of esteem is not the result of an imaginary voyage, which transports us in thought to the most remote times and lands in order to constitute the persons whom we take to be our possible kin, peers, and relatives. "It is not conceivable how a *real* sentiment or passion can ever arise from a known *imaginary* interest. . . ."[17] The moral and social problem is how to go from real sympathies which exclude one another to a real whole which would include these sympathies. The problem is how *to extend* sympathy.

We see the difference between morality and nature, or rather, the lack of adequation between nature and morality. The reality of the moral world requires the constitution of a whole, of a society, that is, the establishment of an invariable system. This reality is not natural, it is artificial. "The rules of justice, in virtue of their universality and absolute inflexibility, cannot be derived from nature, nor can they be the direct creation of a natural inclination or motive."[18]

All the elements of morality (sympathies) are naturally given, but they are impotent by themselves to constitute a moral world. Partialities or particular interests cannot be naturally totalized, because they are mutually exclusive. One can only invent a whole, since the only invention possible is that of the whole. This reveals the essence of the moral problem. Justice is not a principle of nature; it is rather a *rule*, a law of construction, and its role is to organize, within the whole, the elements, including the principles of nature. Justice is a means. The moral problem is the problem of schematism, that is, the act by means of which we refer the natural interests to the *political* category of the whole or to the totality which is not given in nature. The moral world is the artificial totality wherein particular ends are integrated and added to one another. Or again, the moral world is the system of means which allow my particular interest, and also the interest of the other, to be satisfied and realized. Morality may equally well be thought of as a whole in relation to parts and as a means in relation to ends. In short, the moral conscience is a political conscience: true morality is politics, just as the true moralist is the legislator. Expressed in a different way, the moral conscience is a determination of the psychological conscience; it is the psychological conscience apprehended exclusively in the aspect of its inventive power. The moral problem is a problem of the whole and also a problem of means. Legislation is a great invention and the true inventors are not the technologists but rather the legislators. They are not Asclepius and Bacchus but rather Romulus and Theseus.[19]

Now, a system of directed means, a determined whole, is called a rule or a norm. Hume calls it *a general rule*. The rule has two poles: form and content, conversation and property, a system of customs *(moeurs)* and stability of possession. To be in a society is first to substitute possible conversation for violence: the thought of each one represents in itself the thought of the others. But under what conditions? Under the condition that the particular sympathies of each one are transcended in a certain way, and surmount the corresponding partialities or contradictions which they generate among people; or under the condition that natural sympathy can be artificially exercised outside its natural limits. The function of the rule is to determine a stable and common point of view, firm and calm, and independent of our present situation.

> Now, in judging of characters, the only interest or pleasure, which appears the same to every spectator, is that of the person himself, whose character is examin'd; or that of persons, who have a connexion with him.[20]

Undoubtedly, such an interest touches us more feebly than our own, or those of our kin, peers, and relatives; we are going to see that it receives from elsewhere the vividness that it lacks. But at least it has the practical advantage, even when the heart is not in it, of being a general and immutable criterion, a third interest which does not depend on interlocutors—a value.[21] "[E]verything, which gives uneasiness in human action, upon the general survey, is call'd Vice. . . ."[22]

The obligation which is thus created differs essentially from natural obligation, natural and particular interest, or the motive of the action: it is moral obligation or sense of duty. At the other pole, property presupposes similar conditions. "I observe, that it will be for my interest to leave another in the possession of his goods, *provided* he will act in the same manner with regard to me."[23] Here the third interest is a general interest. The convention of property is the artifice by means of which the actions of each one are related to those of the others. It is the establishment of a scheme and the institution of a symbolic aggregate or of the whole. Hume thus finds property to be a phenomenon which is essentially political—in fact, the political phenomenon par excellence. Property and conversation are joined at last, forming the two chapters of a social science.[24] The general sense of the common interest must be *expressed* in order to be efficacious.[25] Reason presents itself here as the conversation of proprietors.

From these first determinations, we can already see that the role of the general rule is twofold, *extensive and corrective*. It corrects our sentiments in making us forget our present situation.[26] At the same time, in terms of its essence, it "goes beyond the circumstance of its birth." Although the sense of duty "[is] deriv'd only from contemplating the actions of others, yet we fail not to extend it even to our own actions."[27] Finally, the rule is that which includes the exception; it makes us sympathize with the other, even when the other does not experience the sentiment which in general corresponds to the situation.

> . . . [A] man, who is not dejected by misfortunes, is the more lamented on account of his patience . . . ; and tho' there be an exception in the present case, yet the imagination is affected by the *general rule*. . . . 'Tis an aggravation of a murder, that it was committed upon persons asleep and in perfect security.[28]

We must, of course, ask how the invention of the rule is possible— indeed, this is the main question. How can we form systems of means, general rules, and aggregates which are both corrective and extensive? But we can already answer the following question: what is it exactly that we invent? In his theory of the artifice, Hume proposes an entire concept of the relation between nature and culture, tendency and institution. Without a doubt, particular interests cannot be made identical to one another, or be naturally totalized. Nonetheless, nature demands that they be made identical. If not, the general rule could never be constituted, property and conversation could not even be conceived of, because sympathies are faced with the following alternative: either to be extended through artifice or to be destroyed through contradiction. As for the passions, they must either be satisfied artificially and obliquely or be snubbed out by violence. As Bentham will explain later on, even more precisely, need is natural, but there is no satisfaction of need, or at least no constant and enduring satisfaction, which is not made possible through artifice, industry, and culture.[29] The identity of interests is therefore artificial, but only in the sense that it eliminates the natural obstacles in the natural identification of the interests themselves. In other words, the significance of justice is exclusively topological. The artifice does not invent a principle other than sympathy. Principles are not invented. The artifice guarantees to sympathy and to natural passions an extension within which they will be capable of being exercised, deployed naturally, and liberated from their natural limits.[30] *Passions are not limited by justice; they are enlarged and extended.* Justice is the extension of the passions and interest, and only the partial movement of the latter is denied and constrained. It is in this sense that *extension* is *correction* and *reflection.*

> There is no passion, therefore, capable of controlling the interested affection, but the very affection itself, by an alteration of its direction. Now this alteration must necessarily take place upon the least reflection.[31]

We must understand that justice is not a reflection *on* interest, but rather a reflection *of* interest, a kind of twisting of the passion itself in the mind affected by it. Reflection is an operation of the tendency which restrains itself. "The remedy, then, is not deriv'd from nature, but from *artifice*; or more properly speaking, nature provides a remedy in the judgment and understanding, for what is irregular and incommodious in the affections."[32] The reflection of tendency is the movement that constitutes practical reason; reason is nothing but a determined moment of the affections of the mind—a calm or rather calmed affection, "grounded in a distinct view or in reflection."

The real dualism, in Hume's work, is not between affection and reason, nature and artifice, but rather between the whole of nature which includes the artifice and the mind affected and determined by this whole. Thus, the fact that the meaning of justice is not reduced to an instinct or to natural obligation does not prevent the existence of moral instinct or natural obligation; above all, it does not prevent the existence of a natural obligation to justice, once the latter is constituted.[33] The fact that esteem does not vary with sympathy, and that it is unlimited, despite the fact that generosity naturally limits itself, does not prevent natural sympathy or limited generosity from being the necessary condition and the only element of esteem: it is because of sympathy that we esteem.[34] That justice is in the final analysis capable, in part, of constraining our passions does not mean that it has an end other than their satisfaction,[35] or another origin other than their determination;[36] it satisfies them obliquely. Justice is not a principle of nature; it is an artifice. But to the extent that humanity is an *inventive species*, even the artifice is nature; the stability of possession is a natural law.[37] As Bergson said, habits are not themselves natural, but what is natural is the habit to take up habits. Nature does not reach its *ends* except by *means* of culture, and tendency is not satisfied except through the institution. History is in this sense part of human nature. Conversely, nature is encountered as the residue of history.[38] Nature is what history does not explain, what cannot be defined, what may even be useless to describe, or what is common in the most diverse ways of satisfying a tendency.

Nature and culture form, therefore, a whole or a composite. Hume repudiates the arguments which assign everything, including justice, to the instinct,[39] and the arguments which assign everything, including the meaning of virtue, to politics and education.[40] The former, as they forget culture, give us a false image of nature; the latter, as they forget nature, deform culture. Above all, Hume centers his critique on the theory of egoism,[41] which is not even a correct psychology of human nature, since it neglects the equally natural phenomenon of sympathy. If by "egoism" we understand the fact that all drives pursue their own satisfaction, we posit only the principle of identity, A = A, that is, the formal and empty principle of a science of humanity—moreover, of an uncultivated and abstract humanity without history and without difference. More specifically, egoism can designate *some* means only that humanity organizes in order to satisfy drives, but not all possible means. Egoism then is put in its place, and this place is no longer very important. At this point one can grasp the sense of Hume's political economy. In the same manner in which he introduces a dimension of sympathy into nature, Hume adds many other motives to interest—motives that are often contradictory (prodigality, ignorance, heredity, custom, habit, or "spirit of greed and endeavor, of luxury and abundance"). *Dispositions are never abstracted from the means which we organize in order to satisfy them.* Indeed, nothing is further from the *homo oeconomicus* than Hume's analysis. History, the true science of human motivation, must denounce the double error of an abstract economy and a falsified nature.

In this sense, the idea that Hume forms of society is very strong. He presents us with a critique of the social contract which not only the utilitarians but also the majority of the jurists opposed to "natural law" would have to take up again. The main idea is this: the essence of society is not the law but rather the institution. The law, in fact, is a limitation of enterprise and action, and it focuses only on a negative aspect of society. The fault of contractual theories is that they present us with a society whose essence is the law, that is, with a society which has no other objective than to guarantee certain preexisting natural rights and no other origin than the contract. Thus, anything positive is taken away from the social, and instead the social is saddled with negativity, limitation, and alienation. The entire Humean critique of the state of nature, natural rights, and the social contract, amounts to the suggestion that the problem must be reversed. The law cannot, by itself, be the source of obligation, because legal obligation presupposes utility. Society cannot guarantee preexisting rights: if people enter society, it is precisely because they do not have preexisting rights. We see clearly in the theory of promise which Hume proposes how utility becomes a principle opposed to the contract.[42] Where is the fundamental difference? Utility is on the side of the institution. The institution, unlike the law, is not a limitation but rather a model of actions, a veritable enterprise, an invented system of positive means or a positive invention of indirect means. This understanding of the institution effectively reverses the problem: outside of the social there lies the negative, the lack, or the need. The social is profoundly creative, inventive, and positive. Undoubtedly, we could say that the notion of convention maintains a great importance in Hume's work. But we must not confuse convention and contract. Placing convention at the base of the institution signifies only that the system of means represented by the institution is a system indirect, oblique, and invented—in a word, cultural. "In like manner are languages gradually etablish'd by human conventions without any promise."[43]

Society is a set of conventions founded on utility, not a set of obligations founded on a contract. Thus, from a social point of view, the law is not primary; it presupposes an institution that it limits. Similarly, the legislator is not the one who legislates, but rather first of all the one who institutes. The problem of the relation between nature and society therefore stands on its head: there is no question any longer of the relation between rights and the law, but rather of needs and institutions. This idea implies an entire remodeling of rights and an original vision of the science of humanity, that is, of the new conception of social psychology. Utility—that is, the relation between institution and need—is therefore a fertile principle: Hume's general rule is an institution. Moreover, if it is the case that the general rule is a positive and functional system finding its own principle in utility, the nature of the link existing between it and the principle of utility must be understood. ". . . [T]ho' the rules of justice are establish'd merely by interest, their connexion with interest is somewhat singular, and is different from what may be observ'd on other occasions."[44]

The fact that nature and society form an indissoluble complex should not make us forget that we cannot reduce society to nature. The fact that humanity is an inventive species does not prevent our inventions from being inventions. Sometimes Utilitarianism is given a "functionalist" interpretation, on the basis of which society is explained by utility, and the institution by drives or needs. Perhaps, there have been writers holding this interpretation, although even this is not certain; at any rate, Hume is not at all the one who held it. It is a fact that a drive is satisfied inside an institution. We speak here of specifically social institutions, not governmental institutions. In marriage, sexuality is satisfied; in property, greed. The institution, being the model of actions, is a designed system of possible satisfaction. The problem is that this does not license us to conclude that the institution is *explained* by the drive. The institution is a system of means, according to Hume, but these means are oblique and indirect; they do not satisfy the drive without also constraining it at the same time. Take, for example, *one* form of marriage, or *one* system of property. Why *this* system and *this* form? A thousand others, which we find in other times and places, are possible. The difference between instinct and institution is this: an institution exists when the means by which a drive is satisfied are not determined by the drive itself or by specific characteristics.

> These words, too, inheritance and contract, stand for ideas infinitely complicated; and to define them exactly a hundred volumes of laws, and a thousand volumes of commentators have not been found sufficient. Does nature, whose instincts in men are all simple, embrace such complicated and artificial objects and create a rational creature without trusting anything to the operation of his reason? . . . All birds of the same species, in every age and country, build their nest alike: in this we see the force of instinct. Men, in different times and places, frame their houses differently: here we perceive the influence of reason and custom. A like inference may be drawn from comparing the instinct of generation and the institution of property.[45]

If nature is the principle of resemblance and uniformity, history is the scene of differences. The drive is general; it does not explain the particular, even when it clearly finds in the particular the form of its satisfaction. "Tho' the establishment of the rule, concerning the stability of possession, be not only useful, but even absolutely necessary to human society, it can never serve to any purpose while it remains in such general terms."[46]

In brief, *utility does not explain the institution.* Private utility does not, since the institution constrains it; nor does public utility fare any better, since it presupposes an entire institutional world that it

CULTURAL WORLD AND GENERAL RULES

cannot create, and to which it is only attached.[47] What could then explain the institution in its essence and in its particular character? Hume has just told us that it is reason and custom; elsewhere he said that it is the imagination, "or the more frivolous properties of our thought and conception."[48] For example, is it or is it not enough in order to become the owner of an abandoned city, to plant one's javelin in its gates?[49] We will not answer the question merely by invoking drives and needs, but rather by examining the relations between drive, circumstance, and imagination. The javelin is the circumstance.

Where the properties of two persons are united

> after such a manner as neither to admit of *division* nor *separation,* as when one builds a house on another's ground, in that case, the whole must belong ... to the proprietor of the most considerable part. ... The only difficulty is, what we shall be pleas'd to call the most considerable part, and most attractive to the imagination. ... The superficies yields to the soil, says the civil law: The writing to the paper: The canvas to the picture. These decisions do not well agree together, and are a proof of the contrariety of those principles, from which they are deriv'd.[50]

Without any doubt, the laws of association regulating the play of the imagination are both the most frivolous and the most serious— the principle of reason and the advantage of the fancy. But for the moment, we need not be concerned with this problem. It suffices, whatever the case, that we anticipate the following: the drive does not explain the institution; what explains it is the *reflection of the drive in the imagination.* We were quick to criticize associationism; we forget too easily that ethnography brings us back to it, and that, as Bergson also says, "among the primitives, we encounter many prohibitions and prescriptions which are explained through a vague association of ideas." And this is not true only for the primitives. Associations are vague, but only in the sense that they are particular and varying according to the circumstances. Imagination is revealed as a veritable production of extremely diverse *models:* when drives are reflected in an imagination submitted to the principles of association, institutions are determined by the figures traced by the drives according to the circumstances. This does not mean that the imagination is in its essence active but only that it *rings out*, and *resonates*. The institution is the figure. When Hume defines feeling, he assigns to it a double function: feeling posits ends and reacts to wholes. These two functions, however, are one: there is feeling when the ends of the drive are also the wholes to which sensibility reacts. But how are these wholes formed? They are formed when the drive and its ends are reflected in the mind. Because human beings do not have instincts, because instincts do not enslave them to the actuality of a pure present, they have liberated the formative power of their imagination, and they have placed their drives in an immediate and direct relation to it. Thus, the satisfaction of human drives is related, not to the drive itself, but rather to the reflective drive. This is the meaning of the institution, in its difference from the instinct. We can then conclude that nature and culture, drive and institution, are one to the extent that the one is satisfied by the other; but they are also two insofar as the latter is not explained by the former.

Similarly, with respect to the problem of justice, the words "schema" and "totality" are entirely justified, since the general rule never indicates particular persons; it does not name owners.

> Justice in her decisions, never regards the fitness or unfitness of objects to particular persons ... the general rule, *that possession must be stable*, is not apply'd by particular judgments, but by other general rules, which must extend to the whole society, and be inflexible either by spite or favour.[51]

We have seen that the rule is *established* by interest and utility, and that it is *determined* by the imagination. In this sense, it does not determine real people; *it is determined* and modified in statements reflecting situations and possible circumstances. This is how the stability of possession is divided between diverse rights: immediate possession, occupation, prescription, accession, succession. But how can the lack of adequation between real persons and possible situations *be corrected?* This lack of adequation may itself be considered a circumstance or a situation. In that case, the mobility of persons will be regulated by the agreed-upon transfer, when the object of the transfer is present or particular, and by the promise, when the object itself is absent or general.[52] We must therefore in the case of the general rule distinguish three dimensions which are nonetheless simultaneous: its *establishment,* its *determination,* and its *correction.*

Yet a difficulty is still present: sympathy, through general rules, has won the constancy, distance, and uniformity of the true moral judgment but has lost in vividness what it has gained in extension. "The consequences of every breach of equity seem to lie very remote, and are not able to counterbalance any immediate advantage, that may be reap'd from it."[53]

The question is no longer how to specify *the rule,* but rather how to provide it with the vividness which it lacks. The question is no longer how to distribute but how to *reinforce* and enliven justice.[54] It was not enough then to single out by means of the imagination the possible situations of the extension of justice; this extension must itself become now a real situation. In an artificial way, the nearest must become the most distant, and the most distant, the nearest. This is the meaning of government. Human beings "cannot change their natures. All they can do is to change their situation, and render the observance of justice the immediate interest of some particular persons, and its violation their more remote."[55]

We find here the principle of all serious political philosophy. True morality does not address itself to children in the family but rather to adults in the state. It does not involve the change of human nature but the invention of artificial and objective conditions in order for the bad aspects of this nature not to triumph. This invention, for Hume, as for the entire eighteenth century, will be political and only political. The governors, "being satisfied with their present situation in the State," apprehend the general interest under the aspect of the immediate and understand justice as the good of their life; for them, the most distant has become the nearest. Conversely, the governed see the nearest become the most distant, to the extent that they have "put it out of their own power, as far as possible, to transgress the laws of society."[56] Government and property are therefore in almost the same relation that belief and abstraction are; in the latter case, the question is about giving roles, and in the former, it is about conferring vivacity. Thus, loyalty completes the list of general rules. At this level, the theory of social contract is criticized once again. There is no question of founding the government on promise, because the promise is an effect of the specification of justice, and loyalty, its support. Justice and government have the same source; they are invented to remedy similar inconveniences: the one simply invents extension, the other, vividness. Being subordinate to justice, the observation of the law of promises is, by the same token and on a different level, the effect of the institution of government, not its cause.[57] The support of justice is therefore independent of its specification, and is produced *on another plane*. Even so, or even more, this support must be determined and distributed in its turn and, like the specification, must, through its correction, make up for its lack of adequation. The specifications of sovereignty will be long possession, accession, conquest, and succession. The correction of sovereignty will be, in rare and precise cases, a certain right to resistance and a certain legitimacy of revolution. We must notice that the permitted revolutions are not political. In fact, the main problem of the state is not a problem of representation, but rather a problem of belief. The state, according to Hume, is not charged with representing the general interest but rather with making the general interest an object of belief. It succeeds in this by giving general interest, mostly through the mechanism of its sanctions, the vividness that only particular interests can have for us naturally. If the rulers, instead of changing their situation, and instead of acquiring an immediate interest in the administration of justice, were to subject the administration of falsified justice to their own immediate passions, then and only then would resistance be legitimate, in the name of a general rule.[58]

Up to now, a first series of rules has given to interest an extension and a generality that interest did not have on its own: through this, possession has turned into property, and stability of possession has been achieved. A second series of rules has given the general rule the presence and vividness that it did not have by itself. But the obstacles which society had to conquer are not only the instability of goods and the abstract character of the general interest. Society is also faced with scarcity of goods.[59] And stability, far from surmounting this obstacle, aggravates it further as it provides possession with conditions favorable for the formation of large properties. Hume often elaborates the idea that, by means of an internal dialectic, property engenders and develops inequality.[60] A third series of rules is therefore necessary to correct both inequality and scarcity. These rules will be the object of political economy. To the stability of possession and loyalty to government, the prosperity of commerce is added at last. The latter "increases industry, by conveying it readily from one member of the state to another, and allowing none of it to perish or become useless."[61]

With respect to Hume's economic theory, only its main theme will be discussed here. Like the two kinds of rules preceding, the prosperity of commerce is also specified and corrected. Its specifications, that is, monetary circulation, capital, interest, and export show its relation with property. Its corrections, on the other hand, show its relation with the state, that is, an accidental relation which comes from outside. Commerce presupposes and involves a preexisting property: from an economic point of view, land rental is primary. The meaning of commerce in general is to guarantee landed property (a political phenomenon) the economic equilibrium that it does not have on its own. The rate of interest gives us a precise example. By itself, "in civilized and populated nations," property puts the class of landowners face to face with the peasant class, the former creating a continuous "demand for borrowing," and the latter not having the money necessary "to supply this demand." The progress of commerce overcomes this contradiction between too many loans and too few riches, in forming a "capitalist interest, and "beget[ting] a number of lenders, and sink[ing] the rate of usury."[62] As for the relation between commerce and the state, we will better understand its principle if we realize that the prosperity of commerce accumulates a working capital allowing for the ease and happiness of the subjects, although the state can always *in case of need* demand and reclaim this capital for itself.

> It is a violent method, and in most cases impracticable, to oblige the labourer to toil, in order to raise from the land more than what subsists himself and family. Furnish him with manufacturers and commodities, and he will do it of himself; afterwards you will find it easy to seize some part of his superfluous labour, and employ it in the public service, without giving him his wonted return.[63]

The state without method or rule acts brusquely and violently. Its actions are repeated accidents imposed upon its subjects, and contrary therefore to human nature. In the methodical state, on the contrary, there appears an entire theory of the accident as the object of corrective rules: this state finds in commerce the possible affirmation of its power and the real condition of its subjects' prosperity; in this way, they both conform to nature.

We have often noticed that in the work of Hume and the utilitarians, economic and political inspiration differ greatly. In his book on utilitarianism,[64] Halévy distinguishes three currents: the natural fusion of interests (sympathies) in ethics; the artificial identification of interests in politics; and the mechanical identity of interests in economics. We have in fact seen how these three currents relate. First of all, we are not confronted with three currents. We should also notice that the mechanics of the economy is no less artificial than the artifice of legislation. Commerce no less than property is an institution; and it presupposes property. But the economy, we are told, has no need of a legislator or of a state. Undoubtedly, this period, at the dawn of the development of capitalism, had not seen or had only sometimes dimly foreseen that the interests of landowners, capitalists, and above all workers do not coincide in one and the same interest. We must, however, seek the germ of such an idea, concrete as it may be in other respects, in an idea which appears frequently in Hume's work. Property, according to him, presents a problem of quantity: goods are scarce, and they are unstable because they are rare. This is the reason why property calls for a legislator and a state. On the contrary, the quantity of money, its abundance or scarcity, does not act on its own: money is the object of a mechanics. We could say that the essential, or perhaps the only theme of Hume's economic essays is to show that the effects which we ordinarily attribute to the quantity of money depend in fact on other causes. What is concrete in this economy is the idea that economic activity involves a qualitative motivation. But sensitive to the difference between commerce and property, from a quantitative point of view, Hume concludes that, in society the quantitative harmony of economic activities is mechanically established, unlike what happens in the case of property.

In view of all this, we can set up the table of general rules or moral categories as follows:

1. Content of the general rule: the stability of possession;

1. Support of the general rule: loyalty to the government;

1. Complement of the general rule: the prosperity of commerce;

2. Specification of the general rules: immediate possession, occupation, etc.;

2. Specification of support: long possession, accession, etc.;

2. Specification of the complement: monetary circulation, capital, etc.;

3. Correction of the preceding specification by means of general rules, promise, transfer.

3. Correction: resistance.

3. Correction: taxes, state service, etc.

THREE

THE POWER OF
THE IMAGINATION
IN ETHICS
AND KNOWLEDGE

SOMETIMES HUME SAYS that the general rule is in essence the combination of reflection and extension. The fact is that the two are identical. The passions are extended because they are reflected; this is the principle of the institution of a rule. But at other times Hume says that we must distinguish between two kinds of non-identical rules, that is, between determining and corrective rules, because the former are more *extensive* than reflective.

> Men are mightily addicted to *general rules*, and . . . we often carry our maxims beyond those reasons, which first induc'd us to establish them. Where cases are similar in many circumstances, we are apt to put them on the same footing, without considering, that they differ in the most material circumstances. . . .[1]

These rules are characterized by the fact that they are extended beyond the circumstances from which they arise. They do not account for the exception, and they misconstrue the accidental, confusing it with the general or the essential: the disadvantages of culture are to be found here. As far as the second kind of rules is concerned, that is, the corrective rules, they are more *reflective* than extensive, precisely because they correct the extension of the determining rules. Instead of confusing the accidental with the general, they present themselves as general rules concerned with the accidental and with the exceptional.

> [G]eneral rules commonly extend beyond the principles, on which they are founded; and . . . we seldom make any exception to them, unless that exception have the qualities of a general rule, and be founded on very numerous and common instances.[2]

Corrective rules express a status of experience that accounts for all possible cases; in the last resort, the exception is a natural thing, and by means of habit and imagination, it becomes the object of experience and knowledge (*savoir*), that is, the object of casuistics.

We are confronted here with two ideas in need of reconciliation: extension and reflection are identical, but they are also different. Two kinds of rules are distinguished, to the extent that they go against each other; nonetheless they have the same origin and share the same principle of constitution. We are thus led back to the main problem: how is the rule possible?

If we begin with unity, the rule is simultaneously the extension and the reflection of the passions. The passions are reflected; but where and in what? They are reflected in the imagination. The general rule is passion as reflected in the imagination. Undoubtedly, the qualities of the passions, being principles of nature, have as their special characteristic affecting and qualifying the mind; but, conversely, the mind reflects its passions and affections.

> [E]verything, which is agreeable to the senses, is also in some measure agreeable to the fancy, and conveys to the thought an image of that satisfaction, which it gives by its real application to the bodily organs.[3]

Being reflected, the passions are found before an enlarged reproduction of themselves, and see themselves liberated from the limits and conditions of their own actuality. They see, therefore, an entire artificial domain opening up, that is, the world of culture; they can project themselves in it through images and deploy themselves without limit. The reflected interest transcends its own partiality. This means that the imagination, filled with the images of the passions and their objects, acquires "a set of passions belonging to it."[4] In reflection, the passions imagine themselves, and the imagination becomes passionate: *the rule is possible.* The real definition of a general rule is that it is a passion of the imagination. "The imagination adheres to the *general* views of Things. . . ."[5]

In this sense, we may distinguish three types of rules. The *rule of taste*, first. We encounter the same problem here in a different form: how does feeling overcome its inconstancy and become an aesthetic judgment? The passions of the imagination do not require efficiency of their object; nor do they require the kind of adaptation which is characteristic of real objects. "These passions are mov'd by degrees of liveliness and strength, which are inferior to *belief*, and independent of the real existence of their objects."[6] Virtue in rags is still virtue; a deserted but fertile soil leads us to think about the happiness of its possible inhabitants. "Sentiments must touch the heart, to make them control our passions: But they need not extend beyond the imagination, to make them influence our taste."[7]

Thus, taste is a feeling of the imagination, not of the heart. It is a rule, and what grounds a rule in general is the distinction between power and the exercise of power. Only the imagination can bring this about, since it reflects both the passions and their object, separating them from their actuality and recuperating them in the mode of the possible. Aesthetics is the science which envisages things and beings under the category of power or possibility. A handsome man in prison for life is the object of an aesthetic judgment, not only because the vigor and balance of his body are separated from their natural exercise and thus simply imagined, but also because the imagination is in this case fascinated by those characteristics.[8] Hume develops this thesis even more precisely in the case of tragedy. The problem here is this: how is it that the spectacle of passions, which are in themselves disagreeable and bleak, can come to delight us? The more the poet knows how to affect, horrify, and make us indignant, "the more [we] are delighted."[9] And, as Hume observes in criticizing a thesis proposed by Fontenelle, it is not enough to say that passions in tragedies are simply fictitious and weakened. This is tantamount to seeing only one side of the solution, the negative and least important side. There is no difference of degree between reality and art; the difference in degree is the condition of a difference in nature. "It is thus the fiction of tragedy softens the passion, by an infusion of a new feeling, not merely by weakening or diminishing the sorrow."[10]

It is not enough for the passion to imagine itself; the imagination must also become passionate at the same time. Tragedy, because it stages an image of passions, provides the spectators' imagination with passions. Just as the reflected interest transcends its partiality, so reflected passions change their quality: the sadness and bleakness of the represented passions are eliminated in the pleasure of the almost infinite play of the imagination. The work of art has therefore its own particular mode of existence, which is not the mode of a real object nor the mode of an actual passion: the lesser degree of belief is the condition for another kind of belief. Artifice has its own belief.

As for the second type of rule—*the rule of freedom*—we feel that the will, which is a kind of passion, "moves easily every way, and produces an image of itself even on that side, on which it did not settle."[11]

Finally, we are faced with *the rule of interest and duty*.

> Two objects may be consider'd as plac'd in this relation, as well when one is the cause of any of the actions or motions of the other, as when the former is the cause of the existence of the latter. . . . A master is such-a-one as by his situation, arising either from force or agreement, has a power of directing in certain particulars the actions of another, whom we call servant.[12]

Hume analyzes with precision one more example of the relation based on duty, that is the relation which links a wife to a husband. As an object to real passion, a wife cannot give to the one who loves perfect certainty and security: anatomy precludes it; the husband can never be sure that the children are his own.[13] Reflected in the imagination, this uncertainty becomes sublimated, takes on a social and cultural content, and appears as the requirement for specifically feminine virtues: a woman, to the extent that she is the object of a possible passion, must always remain chaste, modest, and decent.

> And when a general rule of this kind is once establish'd, men are apt to extend it beyond those principles, from which

it first arose. Thus batchelors, however debauch'd, cannot chuse but be shock'd with any instance of lewdness or impudence in women.[14]

It is therefore the imagination that makes the reflection of passions possible. The general rule is the resonance of an affection in the mind and the imagination. Rules reflect processes and ideas of practice. We must therefore modify our first scheme, which was still too simple. Earlier we saw that the principles of nature and the qualities of passions had to be studied solely in terms of their effect on the mind. However, this effect is only the fact that the imagination is affected and fixed; it is a simple effect. But now we see that we must add a complex effect: the imagination reflects affection, and affection resounds inside the mind. The mind ceases to be fancy, is fixed, and becomes human nature. However, insofar as it reflects the affections which fix it, the mind is still a fancy on another level and in a new way. The fancy is reestablished in the principles of its own transformation, for at least something within the affections escapes all reflection. That which defines the real exercise of the affections, the actuality of their limits, and the action by means of which affections fix the mind in specific forms is precisely that which cannot, without contradiction, allow itself to be reflected. Imagination, as it reflects on the forms of its own stability, liberates these forms, and liberates itself from them; it extends them infinitely. This means that it makes the limit an object of the fancy, it plays with the limit by presenting the accidental as essential, and separates power from its actual exercise. This illusion, says Hume, is an illusion of the fancy.[15] The power of the imagination is to imagine power. In short, the passions do not reflect themselves in the imagination without the imagination extending the passions. The general rule is the absolute unity of the *reflection* of the passions in the imagination and the *extension* of the passions by the imagination. *It is in this sense that reflection and extension are one.*

But it is also in this sense that they are two, since subsequent corrections are necessary in order to establish a rigor in this new domain. This time, the reflection will be a reflection *on* the previous reflection or, if you will, on the reflected interest. But why is it that, in both cases, the same word "reflection" is used? It is because, in our previous discussion, the extension was already a correction: it transcended the partiality of the natural passions. But, because it did not transcend nature without confusing essence and accident, it called for a new correction of, and within, the new, important order it instituted. In fact, it is not enough to think the artifice only through fancy, frivolity, and illusion, for the artifice is also the serious world of culture. The distinction between nature and culture is precisely the distinction between simple and complex effects. Hume, throughout his work, shows a constant interest in the problems of animal psychology, perhaps because the animal is nature without culture: the principles act upon its mind, but their only effect is a simple effect. Not having general rules, being held by the instinct to the actual, lacking any stable fancy and reflective procedures, the animal also lacks history. This is precisely the problem: how to explain that, in the case of humanity, culture and history are constituted in the way that the fancy is reestablished, through the resonance of affections within the mind. *How can we explain this union of the most frivolous and the most serious?*

We have seen that, insofar as the passions are reflected, they necessarily reflect themselves within the fancy. But, in fact, they resonate within a fancy which is already settled, affected, and naturalized. Evidently, the fancy is not settled by the qualities of the passions but rather by those other principles of nature (the modes of association) which operate on a different level. This is the reason why the rule determines itself. Only on this condition, the passions are able to trace effectively constant and determined figures in the imagination. Hume expressly indicates that "nature provides a remedy *in the judgment and understanding,* for what is irregular and incommodious in the affections."[16]

Already in the case of aesthetics, the passions reflect themselves through the principles of association, so that these principles provide a detailed account of the rules of composition: "every kind of composition, is nothing but a chain of propositions and reasonings."[17] Similarly, as we have seen, the rules of property, occupation, accession, and succession are determined through the principles of association:

> A person, who has hunted a hare to the last degree of weariness, wou'd look upon it as an injustice for another to rush in before him, and seize his prey. But the same person, advancing to pluck an apple, that hangs within his reach,

has no reason to complain, if another, more alert, passes him, and takes possession. What is the reason for this difference, but that immobility, not being natural to the hare, but the effect of industry, forms in that case a strong relation with the hunter, which is wanting in the other?[18]

The entire domain of the right is associationist. We expect that an arbitrator or a judge *would apply* the association of ideas and decree to which person or entity a thing is related inside the mind of an observer in general.

> 'Tis the general opinion of philosophers and civilians, that the sea is incapable of becoming the property of any nation; and that because 'tis impossible to take possession of it, or form any such distinct relation with it, as maybe the foundation of property. Where this reason ceases, property immediately takes place. Thus the most strenuous advocates for the liberty of the seas universally allow, that friths and bays naturally belong as an accession to the proprietors of the surrounding continent. These have properly no more bond. or union with the land, than the *pacific* ocean wou'd have; but having an union in the fancy, and being at the same time *inferior*, they are of course regarded as an accession.[19]

In other words, with respect to the determination of the rules of property and with respect to the understanding of history, the imagination makes essential use of the principles of association: in fact, its norm is the easy transition.[20] Thus, the imagination, in the unity that it forms with the simple effect of the principles of association, has really the air of a constitutive imagination: it is quasi-constitutive.

But, one should not forget that, even in this case, it is the fancy which, in the end, invokes the principles of association: having been, in the case of knowledge, settled by the principles, it now uses them to determine and explain in detail the world of culture. One then sees the fundamental link between artifice and fancy, or the part played by the most serious and the most frivolous. ". . . I suspect, that these rules are principally fix'd by the imagination, or the more frivolous properties of our thought and conception."[21]

Moreover, the reasoning that makes up the logical structure of a work is specious and merely plausible; "however disguised by the colouring of the imagination,"[22] it can still be recognized. Behind the determined content of the rules of property and sovereignty, the fancy pokes through; even more clearly, it declares itself in favor of the weaknesses of these rules,[23] or of their mutual oppositions.[24] This is why there are trials, or why juridical discussions can be endless. Thus, in the case of occupation, namely in the case of the city and the javelin, "I find the dispute impossible to be decided . . . because the whole question hangs upon the fancy, which in this case is not possess'd of any precise or determinate standard, upon which it can give sentence."[25]

In the last analysis, the historian is *perplexed*.[26] His perplexity links up with the skepticism of the philosopher and completes it. *This is the reason why the determination of the rule must be corrected*; it must become the object of a second reflection, of a casuistics and a theory of the accidental. We must fill the gap between the principles of the understanding and the new domain where the fancy applies them.

At any rate, the illusion of the fancy is the reality of culture. The reality of culture is an illusion from the point of view of the understanding, but it asserts itself within a domain where the understanding can not, and should not, seek to dissipate illusion. For example, the necessity of an action, such as the understanding conceives it, is neither a quality of the action nor a quality of the agent; it is a quality of the thinking being which considers it. To the extent that we, the agents, in performing the action, can not feel any necessity, we inevitably believe ourselves free.[27] In this sense, the illusion is no less real than the understanding which denounces it; culture is a false experience, but it is also a true experiment. The understanding has the right to exercise its critique only if we unduly transform the powers of culture into real entities, and only if we give real existence to general rules.[28] Otherwise, the understanding can do nothing. It allows its principles of association to be borrowed in order for the world of culture to be determined. In this case, it corrects the extension that these principles assume and composes an entire theory of the exception, although the exception itself forms a part of culture.

The core of the problem is to be found in the relations between passions and the imagination. The determination of these relations constitutes the true originality of the theory of passions. Indeed, what is the simple relation between the imagination and the passions which will permit the latter to develop inside the former a complex effect? The principles of the passions, like the modes of association, transcend the mind and fix it. "Unless nature had given some original qualities to the mind, it cou'd never have any secondary ones; because in that case it wou'd have no foundation for action, nor cou'd ever begin to exert itself."[29]

But the qualities of the passions do not fix the imagination in the way the modes of association do. The modes of association give the ideas possible reciprocal relations, while the qualities of the passions give the relations a direction and a sense; they attribute them with a reality, a univocal movement, and hence with a first term. The self, for example, is the object of pride and humility in virtue of a natural and original property which confers a tendency or a disposition upon the imagination. The idea, or rather the impression of the self, *focuses* the mind.[30] "If a person be my brother I am his likewise: But tho' the relations be reciprocal, they have very different effects on the imagination."[31] The imagination passes easily from the farthest to the nearest, from my brother to me, but not from me to my brother. And here is another example: "men are principally concern'd about those objects, which are not much remov'd either in space or time. . . ."[32]

Moreover, the tendency of the imagination is to move from the present to the future: "We advance, rather than retard our existence."[33] We see how both kinds of affections—relation and passion—situate themselves vis-à-vis each other: association links ideas in the imagination; the passions give a sense to these relations, and thus they provide the imagination with a tendency. It follows, therefore, that the passions need somehow the association of ideas, and conversely, that the association presupposes the passions. Ideas get associated in virtue of a goal, an intention, or a purpose which only the passions can confer upon human activity.[34] We associate our ideas because we have passions. There is therefore a mutual implication between the passions and the association of ideas. " 'Tis observable," says Hume, "of these two kinds of association," that is, of the association of ideas in knowledge and the association of impressions in the passions, "that they very much assist and forward each other. . . ."[35] Thus the imagination follows the tendency which the passions give it; the relation that they suggest, by becoming univocal, has been made real. It is a simple component part, a circumstance of the passions. This is the simple effect of the passions on the imagination. But once again, the imagination is that in which the passions, together with their circumstances, reflect themselves through the principles of association. In this manner, they constitute general rules and valorize things which are very distant, *beyond the tendency of the imagination*. And this is the complex effect: on one hand the possible becomes real, but on the other, the real is reflected.

Are we not, then, at this point capable of solving the problem of the self, by giving a sense to Hume's hope? We are indeed capable of stating what the idea of subjectivity is. The subject is not a quality but rather the qualification of a collection of ideas. To say that the imagination is *affected* by principles amounts to saying that a given collection is qualified as a partial, actual subject. The idea of subjectivity is from then on the reflection of the affection in the imagination *and the general rule itself*. The idea is no longer here the object of a thought or the quality of a thing; it is not representational. It is a governing principle, a schema, a rule of construction. Transcending the partiality of the subject whose idea it is, the idea of subjectivity includes within each collection under consideration the principle and the rule of a possible agreement between subjects. Thus, the problem of the self, insoluble at the level of the understanding, finds, uniquely within culture, a moral and political solution. We saw that origin and affection could not be combined within the self because, at this level, there subsists a great difference between principles and the fancy. That which constitutes now the self is the synthesis of the affection and its reflection, the synthesis of an affection which fixes the imagination and of an imagination which reflects the affection.

Practical reason is the establishment of a whole of culture and morality. That this whole can be presented in detail does not contradict this statement, because it is a detail of general determinations and not of parts.[36] How can this whole be established? The *schematizing imagination* makes it possible, to the extent that the schematism manifests and translates three properties of the imagination: imagination is reflective, essentially excessive, and quasi-constitutive. But, at the other end, theoretical reason is the determination of the detail of nature, that is, of parts submitted to calculation.

How is this determination possible? Surely it is not possible the way the establishment of the whole of culture and morality is, for we have seen that the system of the understanding and the system of morality do not represent parallel affections of the mind. Therefore a schematism must exist which is peculiar to theoretical reason. Schematism, in this case, would no longer be the principle of construction of a whole but rather the principle of the determination of parts. The role of the principles of association is to fix the imagination. But association, unlike the passions, has no need to be reflected in order to calm itself, or in order to constitute reason. It is immediately calm, and "operates secretly and calmly on the mind."[37]

In this sense, reason is imagination that has become nature; it is the totality of the simple effects of association, general ideas, substances, and relations. But then, since there are two kinds of relations, there are two kinds of reason. In the case of the relations between ideas, we must distinguish between those that "depend entirely on the ideas which we compare together" (resemblance, relations of quantity, degrees of quality, contrariety) and the relations of objects, which "may be chang'd without any change in the ideas" (relations of time and place, identity, causality).[38] Similarly, we must distinguish between two kinds of reason: the reason that proceeds on the basis of *certainty* (intuition and demonstration)[39] and the reason that proceeds in terms of probabilities[40] (experimental reason, *understanding*).[41] Undoubtedly, these two kinds of reason are merely two different uses of reason, in view of two kinds of relations, and must have a common root—*comparison*. It would seem to follow that the convictions they generate (certainty and belief) are not without relation to each other,[42] despite the fact that they remain distinct. For example, once we have shown that causality is not the object of certainty or knowledge, the question remains whether or not the understanding, whose object it is, produces it,[43] or whether or not causality is derived from probability.[44] The answer to this last question would still be negative, but the arguments which support this new negation lead us, at the same time, to understand the difference between the two dimensions of reason.

The principle from which the causal relation is derived as an effect has a gradual formation. *Here, human nature does not by itself produce its effect.* "[C]an any one give the ultimate reason, why past experience and observation produces such an effect, any more than why nature alone shou'd produce it?"[45] According to Hume, human nature takes the detour of the observation of nature, or of an experience of nature—and this is the essential. "As the habit, which produces the association, arises from the frequent conjunction of objects, it must arrive at its perfection by degrees, and must acquire new force from each instance, that falls under our observation."[46]

We can see clearly at this point why causality cannot be derived from probability.[47] Actually, we must designate every determined degree of habit as a probability,[48] without forgetting that probability presupposes habit as a principle. This presupposition is based on the fact that each degree of habit is, in relation to an object, the mere presumption of the existence of another object, like the one which *habitually* accompanies the first object.[49] The paradox of habit is that it is formed by degrees and also that it is a principle of human nature: "habit is nothing but one of the principles of nature, and derives all its force from that origin."[50]

The principle is the habit of contracting habits. A gradual formation, to be specific, is a principle, as long as we consider it in a general way. In Hume's empiricism, genesis is always understood in terms of principles, and itself as a principle. To derive causality from probability is to confuse the gradual formation of a principle upon which reason depends with the progress of reasoning. In fact, experimental reason is the result of habit—and not vice versa. Habit is the root of reason, and indeed the principle from which reason stems as an effect.[51]

In its other use, however, that is, in the domain of the relations of ideas, reason is determined immediately by the corresponding principles, without a gradual formation and under the sole influence of human nature. The famous texts on mathematics have precisely this provenance.[52] Similarly, the definition of the relations of ideas, "in the case in which the relations depend entirely on ideas that we compare to one another," *does not mean that association is here, more than elsewhere, a quality of the ideas themselves,* nor that mathematics is a system of analytic judgments. Whether as relations of ideas or as relations of objects, relations are always external to their terms. What Hume means is this: principles of human nature produce in the mind relations of ideas as they act "on their own" on ideas. This is different from what happens in the case of the three relations between objects, where the very observation of nature acts as a principle. To the logic of mathematics, which we shall discuss later on, there must therefore be juxtaposed a logic of physics or of existence, and only general rules will bring about the latter effectively.[53] *From the point of view of relations* only physics is the object of a schematism.[54]

To say that a principle of nature—in this case, habit—is formed gradually is to say, in the first place, that experience is itself a principle of nature.

> Experience is a principle, which instructs me in the several conjunctions of objects for the past. Habit *is another principle*, which determines me to expect the same for the future; and both of them conspir[e] to operate upon the imagination. . . .[55]

We must also note that habit is a *principle different from* experience, although it also presupposes it. As a matter of fact, the habit I adopt will never by itself explain the fact that I adopt a habit; a repetition will never by itself form a progression. Experience causes us to observe particular conjunctions. Its essence is the repetition of similar cases. Its effect is causality as a philosophical relation. This is how imagination turns into understanding. However, this does not yet explain how the understanding is able to make an inference or to *reason* about causes and effects. The real content of causality—registered by the term "always"—cannot be constituted in experience, because, in a sense, it constitutes experience.[56] One instance of reasoning does not render reasoning possible; nor is reasoning immediately given in the understanding. The understanding must, from a principle other than experience, derive the faculty of drawing conclusions from experience, and also of transcending experience and making inferences. Repetition by itself does not constitute progression, nor does it form anything. The repetition of similar cases does not move us forward, since the only difference between the second case and the first is that the second comes after the first, without displaying a new idea.[57] Habit is not the mechanics of quantity. "Had ideas no more union in the fancy than objects seem to have to the understanding, we cou'd never draw any inference from causes to effects, nor repose belief in any matter of fact."[58]

This is the reason why habit appears as another principle, and causality as a natural relation or as an association of ideas.[59] The effect of this other principle is to turn imagination into belief,[60] thanks to the transition made from the impression of an object to the idea of another. Thus, a double implication is sketched out. On one hand, habit allows the understanding to reason about experience, as it transforms belief into a possible act of the understanding. ". . . [M]emory, senses, and understanding," says Hume, "are, therefore, all of them founded on the imagination or the vivacity of our ideas."[61] On the other hand, habit presupposes experience: once their conjunction is discovered, objects are linked together in the imagination. We could even say that habit is experience, insofar as it produces the idea of an object by means of the imagination and not by means of the understanding.[62] Repetition becomes a progression, or even a production, when we no longer see it in relation to the objects repeated, because, if we do, it changes, discovers and produces nothing. It becomes a production as soon as we see it from the point of view of the mind which contemplates it, for it produces a new impression in it, "a determination to carry our thoughts from one object to another"[63] and "to transfer the past to the future,"[64] that is, an anticipation or a tendency. The fact is that experience and habit are two different principles; they stand alternatively for the presentation of cases of constant conjunction to the inspecting mind, and for the union of these cases inside the mind which observes them. Because of this, Hume always gives causality two related definitions: causality is the union of similar objects and also a mental inference from one object to another.[65]

An analogy seems to be imposed between artifice (moral world) and habit (world of knowledge). These two instances, inside their corresponding worlds, are at the origin of general rules which are both extensive and corrective. But they do not function in the same way. In the system of morality, the rules are invited to reflect in general the principles of nature in the imagination. But, in the system of knowledge, the condition of these rules is located in the very particular character of a principle, not only insofar as it presupposes experience (or something equivalent to experience) but also insofar as it must be formed. Yet we would say that naturally this formation has its own laws which define the legitimate exercise of a reasoning understanding. We have seen that the formation of a principle was the principle of a formation. Belief, says Hume, is the effect of the principles of a prudent nature.[66] The idea we believe is, by definition, the idea associated with a present impression, the idea therefore that fixes the imagination, or the idea to which the impression communicates its vividness. This communication is undoubtedly reinforced through resemblance and contiguity,[67] but it finds its law essentially in causality and habit. In the final analysis it finds its law in the repetition of cases of constant conjunction of two objects observed through experience. However, this is precisely where the difficulty lies. *Habit itself is a principle different from experience; the unity of experience and habit is not given.*

By itself, habit can feign or invoke a false experience, and bring about belief through "a repetition" which "is not deriv'd from experience."[68] This will be an illegitimate belief, *a fiction of the imagination.* "The custom of imagining a dependence has the same effect as the custom of observing it wou'd have."[69] Thus, the imagination will not allow itself to be fixed by the principle of habit, without at the same time using habit for the purpose of passing off its own fancies, transcending its fixity and going beyond experience. "... [T]his habit not only approaches in its influence, but even on many occasions prevails over that which arises from the constant and inseparable union of causes and effects."[70]

Beliefs produced in this manner, albeit illegitimate from the point of view of a rigorous exercise of the understanding, no matter how inevitable that may be, form the set of general, extensive, and excessive rules that Hume calls *nonphilosophical probability.* "An Irishman cannot be witty, a Frenchman cannot have solidity." Hence, despite first appearances, the understanding cannot count upon nature for the immediate determination of the laws of its legitimate exercise. These laws can only be the product of correction and reflection; the second series of general rules will stem from them. Only when the understanding, through a new operation, resumes the act of belief and holds it together with its principle within the limits of past experience will the legitimate conditions of belief be recognized and applied; only then will they form the rules of *philosophical probability* or the calculus of probabilities. (In this sense, the extensive rules of the passions, in the moral world, must be corrected as soon as they have been determined by the principles of association. They must be corrected not only because, as it happens, these principles have been involved and activated by the fancy on a level which was not their own; they must be corrected because causality has already, by itself and on its own level, a fanciful, extensive use. The understanding *is able* to correct the extensive rules of the passions and to question itself on the nature of morality, because it *must* first of all correct the extension of knowledge itself.)

Illegitimate beliefs or repetitions which are not based on experience, as well as nonphilosophical probabilities, have two sources: language and the fancy. *These are fictitious causalities.* Language, by itself, produces belief, as it substitutes observed repetition with spoken repetition, and the impression of a present object with the hearing of a specific word which allows us to conceive ideas vividly. "[W]e have a remarkable propensity to believe whatever is reported, even concerning apparitions, enchantments, and prodigies, however contrary to daily experience and observation."[71]

The philosopher, having spoken continuously of faculties and occult qualities, ends up believing that these words "have a secret meaning, which we might discover by reflection."[72] The liar, having continuously repeated his own lies, ends up believing them.[73] Not only is credulity thus explained by the power of words, but also education,[74] eloquence, and poetry.[75]

> We have been so much accusom'd to the names of MARS, JUPITER, VENUS, that in the same manner as education infixes any opinion, the constant repetition of these ideas makes them enter into the mind with facility, and prevail upon the fancy. . . . The several incidents of the piece acquire a kind of relation by being united into one poem or representation; . . . and the vivacity produc'd by the fancy is in many cases greater than that which arises from custom and experience.[76]

In brief, words produce a "phantom of belief,"[77] or a "counterfeit,"[78] which renders the most severe critique of language philosophically necessary. Moreover, the fancy makes us confuse the essential and the accidental. In fact, the counterfeit character of beliefs depends always on an accidental characteristic: it depends not on the relations between objects but on "the present temper and disposition of the person."[79] The fancy interprets the appearance of merely accidental circumstances accompanying an object as the repetition of this object within experience.[80] Thus, for example, in the case of a man suffering from vertigo, "the circumstances of depth and descent strike so strongly upon him, that their influence cannot be destroy'd by the contrary circumstances of support and solidity, which ought to give him a perfect security."[81]

Thus, in the field of the understanding and in the field of morality, the imagination is essentially exceeding. However, we can see the difference. When knowledge is exceeded, we no longer find the positivity of art; we find only the negativity of errors and lies. This is the reason why correction will no longer be the institution of a qualitative rigor, but rather the denunciation of error with the help of a calculus of quantities. In the world of knowledge, and in the case of the understanding, extensive rules are no longer the obverse of a reflection *of* the principles in the imagination; they only translate the impossibility of a preventive reflection bearing *on* the principle. "... [W]hen we have been accustom'd to see one object united to another, our imagination passes from the first to the second, by a natural transition, which precedes reflection, and which cannot be prevented by it."[82]

The imagination is able to believe only by falsifying belief in the confusion of the accidental and the general. Habit is a principle which cannot invoke experience without falsifying it, or without, at the same time, invoking fictitious repetitions. Hence, the necessity of an ulterior reflection which can only present itself as a correction, a subtraction, a second kind of rules, or as a criterion for a quantified distinction between the general and the accidental. "... [T]hese rules are form'd on the nature of our understanding, and on our experience of its operations in the judgments we form concerning objects."[83]

The object of philosophical probability or of the calculus of probabilities is to maintain belief within the limits of the understanding and to ensure conformity between habit and experience. Habit and experience are the means by which fictions and prejudices are dissipated. In other words, reasoning, in order to be absolutely legitimate, must be born of habit "not *directly* ... but in an *oblique* manner."[84] Undoubtedly, the characteristic of belief, inference, and reasoning is to transcend experience and to transfer the past to the future; but it is still necessary that the object of belief be determined in accordance with a past experience. Experience is *partes extra partes*; objects are separated in the understanding. "... [W]hen we transfer the past to the future, the known to the unknown, every past experiment has the same weight, and ... 'tis only a superior number of them, which can throw the balance on any side."[85]

71

We must determine the number of past experiences, and also the opposition between parts and their quantitative agreement. To believe is an act of the imagination, in the sense that the concordant images presented by the understanding or the concordant parts of nature ground themselves upon one and the same idea in the *imagination*. This idea must still find its content and also the measure of its vividness, in the greatest number of similar parts offered separately by the *understanding*.[86]

The necessity of a critique of rules by rules is therefore confirmed. The difficulty is that both kinds of rule, extensive and corrective, nonphilosophical and philosophical probability, insofar as they "are in a manner set in opposition to each other,"[87] are the effect of one and the same principle: habit. They have the same origin. "The following of general rules is a very unphilosophical species of probability; and yet 'tis only by following them that we can correct this, and all other unphilosophical probabilities."[88]

However, because habit is not, in itself and by itself, confined to the repetition of cases observed within experience, since other repetitions can form it equally well, the adequation between habit and experience is a scientific result that must be obtained, and the object of a task that must be accomplished. This task is accomplished to the extent that the act of belief bears exclusively upon an object being determined in accordance with the nature of the understanding, and in accordance with repetitions observed in experience.[89] This determination constitutes the sense of corrective rules; the latter recognize causality in the detail of nature, they allow us to know when objects "become causes or effects,"[90] and they denounce, as a consequence, illegitimate beliefs.[91] In brief, habit has opposite effects upon the imagination and on the judgment: on one hand, extension, *and on the other*, the correction of this extension.[92]

FOUR

GOD AND
THE WORLD

IF WE WERE to look for an example which would bring together all
the significations that we have successively attributed to general rules,
we would find it in religion. Four kinds of rule must be distinguished:
extensive and corrective rules of passions, and extensive and corrective rules of knowledge. Now, religion participates equally in knowledge and in passion. In fact, religious feeling has two poles: polytheism and theism. The two corresponding sources are the qualities
of the passions and the modes of association, respectively.[1] Theism
has its source in the unity of the spectacle of nature, in other words,
in the sort of unity which only resemblance and causality can guarantee in phenomena. Polytheism has its source in the diversity of
the passions and the irreducibility of successive passions.

Furthermore, religion, in each of these cases, is presented as a
system of extensive rules. Although the religious feeling finds its
source in the passions, it is not itself a passion. It is not an instinct,
says Hume, nor a primitive impression of nature. Unlike self-esteem
or sexuality, it is not naturally determined; rather it is a subject of
historical study.[2] The gods of polytheism are the echo, the extension,
and the reflection of the passions, and their heaven is our imagination
only. In this sense, we encounter once more the characteristic of the
extensive rule: religious feeling confuses the accidental with the

essential. Its origin is in the events of human life, in the diversity
and the contradiction we find in it, and in the alternation of happiness
and unhappiness, of hopes and fears.[3] The religious feeling is awakened in the strange encounters which we make in the sensible world,
and in the exceptional and fantastic circumstances or the unknown
phenomena which we (mis)take for essence, precisely because they
are unknown.[4] This confusion defines superstition and idolatry. "*Bar-
barity, caprice*; these qualities, however nominally disguised, we may
universally observe, form the ruling character of the deity in popular
religions."[5]

Idolaters are people of "artificial lives,"[6] the ones who make an
essence out of the extraordinary, the ones who look for "an immediate service of the Supreme Being." They are the mystics, the
fanatics, and the superstitious. Such souls throw themselves volun-
tarily into criminal adventures, because their common denominator
is that moral acts are not enough for them. Morality is joyless—after
all, morality is not picturesque; prestige belongs to vice: "Men are
even afraid of passing for good-natur'd; lest *that* should be taken for
want of understanding: And often boast of more debauches than
they have been really engag'd in. . . ."[7]

But on the other hand, at the other pole, theism is also a system
of extensive rules. This time, though, the extension under consideration is an affair of knowledge. Religion is, in this sense again, a
kind of overstride of the imagination, a fiction, and a simulacrum of
belief. It invokes a spoken repetition and an oral or written tradition.
The priests speak and the miracles rest on human testimony;[8] however, the miracles do not immediately manifest a reality, but claim
for themselves the fitness that, generally, we are accustomed to find
between testimony and reality. Or again, in the proofs for the existence of God that are based on *analogy* between machines and the
world, religion confuses the general and the accidental. It does not
see that the world has but an extremely distant resemblance to machines, and that it resembles them only in terms of the most accidental circumstances.[9] Why take human technical activity as the
base for the analogy, rather than another mode of operation—no
more and no less partial—such as, for example, generation or vegetation?[10] Finally, in the proofs based on *causality*, religion transcends
the limits of experience. It aspires to prove God by His effect, that
is, the world or nature. But then sometimes, as in the case of

Cleanthes,[11] religion blows the effect out of all proportion, totally denying disorder or the presence and intensity of evil, by constituting God as an adequate cause of a world which it arbitrarily embellishes. At other times, as in the case of Demea,[12] religion accords more with the cause and establishes a disproportionate God. In the end, it redescends to earth and remedies the lack of adequation by invoking unknown effects, the most important of which is future life. It is evident that religion misuses the principle of causality. In fact, there is no usage of causality in religion that is not illegitimate and fictitious.

> It is only when two *species* of objects are found to be constantly conjoined, that we can infer the one from the other; and were an effect presented, which was entirely singular, and could not be comprehended under any known *species*, I do not see, that we could form any conjecture or inference at all concerning its cause.[13]

In other words, there are no physical objects or objects of repetition except in the world. The world as such is essentially the Unique. It is a fiction of the imagination—never an object of the understanding. Cosmologies are always fanciful. Thus, in Hume's texts, in a manner that differs from Kant's, the theory of causality has two stories to tell: the determination of the conditions of a legitimate exercise in relation to experience, and the critique of illegitimate exercise outside experience.

Religion, then, is a dual system of extensive rules. But how could it be corrected? We understand easily that its situation, in knowledge and culture, is very particular. Undoubtedly, the correction exists. The miracle is subordinated to the world of knowledge: the evidence drawn from testimony, to the extent that it claims to belong to experience, becomes a probability entering calculations. It becomes one of the two terms of an abstraction, whereas the other stands for contrary evidence.[14] In culture or in the moral world, corrective rules, instead of confounding the exception, recognize it and include it, creating thereby a theory of experience wherein all possible cases find a rule of intelligibility and get to be ordered under a statute of the understanding. In one of his essays, Hume analyzes an example of this theory of the exception: suicide is not a transgression of our duties toward God, nor of our duties toward society. Suicide is within human powers, and no more impious an act than "to build houses"; it is a power which should be used in exceptional circumstances.[15] The exception therefore becomes an object of nature. "Do you imagine that I repine at Providence, or curse my creation, because I go out of life, and put a period to a being which, were it to continue, would render me miserable?"[16]

But the question now is the following: as religion is corrected, what is really left of it? In both cases, correction seems to be a total critique; it does not allow anything to subsist. Nothing is left of the miracle; it disappears in an abstraction without proportion. The figures of the extension which we have previously studied—justice, government, commerce, art, mores, even freedom—had a positivity of their own, confirmed and reinforced as they were by the corrections; they formed the world of culture. On the other hand, Hume seems to exclude religion from culture, and all that goes with it. When, in religion, words consecrate an object, while in the social and legal spheres promising words change the nature of actions relative to some other objects, the sense is not the same.[17] Philosophy is reaching completion here in a practical battle against superstition.

At the other pole, the corrective rules which make true knowledge possible by giving criteria and laws for its exercise do not act without expelling from the domain they define every fictitious usage of causality; and they begin with religion. In brief, it seems that, in the domain of the extension, religion keeps only frivolity and loses all seriousness. We understand why. Religion is indeed the extension of passions and their reflection in the imagination. But in religion, the passions are not reflected in an imagination already settled by the principles of association in a way that would make seriousness possible. On the contrary, there is religion only when these principles are reflected in pure imagination and mere fancy. Why is that? Because religion, by itself and in its other aspects, is *only* the fanciful usage of the principles of association, resemblance, and causality.

Is nothing therefore left of religion? If this were the case, how could we explain the final reversal of the essay "On the Immortality of the Soul" and "The Essay on Miracles"? To believe in miracles is a false belief, but it is also a true miracle.

And whoever is moved by *Faith* to assent to it, is conscious of a continued miracle in his own person, which subverts

all the principles of his understanding, and gives him a determination to believe what is most contrary to custom and
experience.[18]

The irony of Hume and his necessary precautions may be invoked
at this point. But even if it is correct to do so, it will not explain
the properly philosophical content of the *Dialogues*. In fact, religion
is justified, but only in its very special situation, outside culture and
outside true knowledge. We have seen that philosophy has nothing
to say on what causes the principles and on the origin of their power.
There, it is the place of God. We cannot make use of the principles
of association in order to know the world as an effect of divine
activity, and even less to know God as the cause of the world; but
we can always think of God negatively, as the cause of the principles.
It is in this sense that theism is valid, and it is in this sense that
purpose is reintroduced. Purpose will be thought, albeit not known,
*as the original agreement between the principles of human nature and nature
itself.* "There is a kind of pre-established harmony between the course
of nature and the association of our ideas."[19]

*Purpose gives us therefore, in a postulate, the originary (originelle) unity
of origin and qualification.* The idea of God, as originary agreement,
is the thought of something in general; as for knowledge, it can only
find content in self-mutilation, after being identified with a certain
mode of appearance that experience manifests, or after being determined by means of an analogy which will necessarily be partial. "In
this little corner of the world alone, there are four principles, *reason*,
instinct, generation, vegetation,"[20] and each one of them can furnish
us with a coherent discourse on the origin of the world. But if the
origin as such is thought but not known, if it is all these things at
the same time—matter and life as much as spirit—it is bound to be
indifferent to every opposition; it is beyond good and evil.[21] Each
one of the perspectives we have of it has only one function—to make
us transcend the other perspectives which are equally possible, and
to remind us that we are always confronted with partial analogies.
In certain respects, purposiveness is more an *élan vital*, and less the
project or the design of an infinite intelligence.[22] One could object
here that all order arises from a design; but that would be to suppose
the problem solved,[23] to reduce all purposiveness to an intention,
and to forget that reason is but one *modus operandi* among others.
"Why an orderly system may not be spun from the belly as well as

from the brain[?]."[24] In this new state of affairs, what does the Idea of the World become? Is it still a simple fiction of the fancy?

We have already seen two fictitious uses of the principle of causality. The first was defined by repetitions which do not proceed from experience; the second, by a particular object—the world—which cannot be repeated, and which is not, properly speaking, an object. Now, according to Hume, there is also a third, fictitious or excessive causality. It is manifested in the belief in the distinct and continuous existence of bodies. On one hand, we attribute *a continuous existence* to objects, in virtue of a type of causal reasoning which has as its ground the coherence of certain impressions.[25] Despite the discontinuity of my perceptions, I admit "the continu'd existence of objects in order to connect their past and present appearances, and give them such an union with each other, as I have found by experience to be suitable to their particular natures and circumstances."[26]

This is then the resolution of the contradiction that would arise between the conjunction of two objects in actual experience and the appearance of one of them only in my perception, without the appearance of its counterpart.[27] But this resolution is based on a mere fiction of the imagination: the inference is fictitious and the causal reasoning, extensive. It transcends the principles that determine the conditions of its legitimate exercise in general and maintain it within the bounds of the understanding. In fact, I confer to the object more coherence and regularity than what I find in my perception.

> But as all reasoning concerning matters of fact arises only from custom, and custom can only be the effect of repeated perceptions, the extending of custom and reasoning beyond the perceptions can never be the direct and natural effect of the constant repetition and connexion.[28]

On the other hand, *distinct existence* rests on an equally false use of causality, that is, on a fictitious and contradictory causality. We affirm a causal relation between the object and our perception of it, but never do we seize the object independently of the perception that we have of it. We forget that causality is legitimized only when past experience reveals to us the conjunction of *two* entities.[29] In short, continuity and distinctness are outright fictions and illusions of the imagination, since they revolve around, and designate that which, by definition, is not offered to any possible experience, either through the senses or through the understanding.

It seems that all of this transforms the belief in continuous and distinct existence into a specific case of the extensive rule. At first glance, the texts which are about the constitution of this belief and the texts which are about the formation of rules seem to parallel each other. The imagination always makes use of the principles which fix it, that is, of contiguity, resemblance, and causality, in order to transcend its limits, and to extend these principles beyond the conditions of their exercise.[30] Thus, the coherence of changes causes the imagination to feign yet more coherence, as it comes to admit continuous existence.[31] This constancy and resemblance of appearances cause the imagination to attribute to similar appearances the identity of an invariable object. In this way, the imagination feigns once again continuous existence in order to overcome the opposition between the identity of resembling perceptions and the discontinuity of appearances.[32] The fact is, though, that this parallelism between belief and rule is only apparent. The two problems, although they are very different, complement each other. Contrary to extensive rules, the fiction of continuity is not corrigible, it cannot and should not be corrected. It maintains, therefore, different relations with reflection. Moreover, as far as the imagination is concerned, its origin is very different from that of general rules.

We begin with the second point. Extensive rules can be distinguished from the belief in the existence of bodies by means of two characteristics. First of all, the object of the extensive rules of knowledge is a particular determination to which the imagination confers the value of a law. It does so by borrowing, from the principles which fix it, the power to go beyond principles; and it succeeds in this by invoking an alleged experience or, in other words, by offering the understanding a mere item of fancy, as though it were an object which concerned it. Imagination offers the understanding as a general, elaborate experience, the purely accidental content of an experience that only the senses have registered in chance encounters. On the other hand, the imagination does not present to the understanding continuous and distinct existence as an object of possible experience; nor does the understanding denounce the use of it by the imagination as the object of a false experience. Undoubtedly, there is no experience of continuous existence either through the senses or through the understanding, because continuous existence is not a particular object; it is the characteristic of the World in general. It is not an object because it is the horizon which every object presupposes. (Of course, we have already seen this in the case of religious belief. But being more than an extensive rule, religious belief appears now as something composite, made up of rules and the belief in the existence of bodies. It participates in the rules to the extent that it treats the world as a particular object and invokes an experience of the senses and of the understanding.)

Second, on the basis of the belief in the existence of bodies, *fiction becomes a principle of human nature.* The most important point is to be found here. The entire sense of the principles of human nature is to transform the *multiplicity* of ideas which constitute the mind into a *system,* that is, a system of knowledge and of its objects. But for a system to exist, it is not enough to have ideas associated in the mind; it is also necessary that perceptions be regarded as separate from the mind, and that impressions be in some manner torn from the senses. We must give the object of the idea an existence which does not depend on the senses. The objects of knowledge must truly be objects. To that end, the principles of association do not suffice, no more than the vividness of impressions or a mere belief does. The system is complete when "a seeming interruption" of an appearance to the senses is surpassed "by [the] feigning [of] a continu'd being which may fill those intervals, and preserve a perfect and entire identity to our perceptions."[33]

In other words, the system is completed in the identity between system and world. But, as we have seen, the system is the product of the principles of nature, whereas the world (continuity and distinction) is an outright fiction of the imagination. Fiction becomes principle necessarily. In the case of general rules, fiction draws its origin and its force from the imagination, insofar as the latter makes use of principles which fix it, and allow it therefore to go further. In the case of the belief in continuity, the force of fiction is the force of a principle. *With the World, the imagination has truly become constitutive and creative.* The World is an Idea. Undoubtedly, Hume always presents continuity as an excessive effect of causality, resemblance, and contiguity, and as the product of their illegitimate extension.[34] But, in fact, contiguity, resemblance, and causality do not, properly speaking, intervene as principles; they are the characteristics of certain impressions—precisely those impressions which will be lifted from the senses in order to constitute the world.[35] What is treated as a principle is the belief in the existence of bodies, along with the ground on which this belief depends.[36]

The belief in the existence of bodies includes several moments: first, it includes the principle of identity, as a product of the fiction by means of which the idea of time is applied to an invariable and continuous object; then, it includes the confusion by means of which an earlier identity is attributed to similar impressions; this confusion is due to the easy transition (itself an effect of resemblance) that resembles the effect created by the consideration of the identical object; then one more fiction is included—that of continuous existence—which serves to overcome the contradiction between the discontinuity of impressions and the identity we attribute to them.[37] And this is not all. It may indeed seem bizarre that Hume, in the space of a few pages, first presents as satisfactory the conciliation brought about by the fiction of a continuous existence,[38] and then again as false and as dragging along with it other fictions and other conciliations.[39] The reason is that continuous existence is very easily reconciled with the discontinuity of appearances. It can therefore legitimately tie together discontinuous images and the perfect identity which we attribute to them. It is a fact that the attribution of identity is false, that our perceptions are really interrupted, and that the affirmation of a continuous existence hides an illegitimate usage of the principles of human nature. To make things worse, *this usage is itself a principle.* The opposition then is at its innermost state in the center of the imagination. The difference [between] imagination and reason has become a contradiction.

> The imagination tells us, that our resembling perceptions
> have a continu'd and uninterrupted existence, and are not
> annihilated by their absence. Reflection tells us, that even
> our resembling perceptions are interrupted in their existence,
> and different from each other.[40]

This contradiction, says Hume, is established between extension and reflection, imagination and reason, the senses and the understanding.[41] In fact, this way of phrasing the issue is not the best, since it can apply to general rules as well. Elsewhere, Hume says it more clearly: the contradiction is established between the *principles of the imagination and the principles of reason.*[42] In the preceding chapters, we have constantly shown the opposition between reason and imagination, or between human nature and the fancy. We have seen successively how the principles of human nature fix the imagination; how the imagination resumes its operation beyond this fixation; and lastly how reason comes to correct this resumption. But the problem now is that the opposition has really become a contradiction: at the last moment, the imagination is recuperated on a precise point. But this last moment is also the first time. For the first time, the imagination is opposed, *as a principle*, that is, as a principle of the world, to the principles which fix it and to the operations which correct it. To the extent that fiction, along with the World, count among the principles, the principles of association encounter fiction, and are opposed to it, without being able to eliminate it. The most internal opposition is now established between constituted and constitutive imagination, between the principles of association and the fiction which has become a principle of nature.

It is precisely because fiction or extension has become a *principle*, that it can no longer be included, corrected, and even less eliminated through reflection.[43] We need a new relation between extension and reflection. This is no longer the relation offered by the popular system which affirms continuous existence, but rather the relation offered by the philosophical system which affirms distinct and independent existences: objects are distinct from perceptions, perceptions are discontinuous and perishable, objects are "uninterrupted, and . . . preserve a continu'd existence and identity."[44] "This hypothesis . . . pleases our reason, in allowing, that our dependent perceptions are interrupted and different; and at the same time is agreeable to the imagination, in attributing a continu'd existence to something else, which we call *objects*."[45]

But this aesthetic game of the imagination and reason is not a reconciliation; it is rather the persistence of a contradiction, whose terms we alternately embrace.[46] Moreover, it ushers in its own difficulties, involving, as we have seen, a new and illegitimate usage of causality.[47] The philosophical system is not initially recommended to reason or to the imagination. It is "the monstrous offspring of two principles . . . which are both at once embrac'd by the mind, and which are unable mutually to destroy each other."[48] This system is a delirium. When fiction becomes principle, reflection goes on reflecting, but it can no longer correct. It is thus thrown into delirious compromises.

From the point of view of philosophy, the mind is no longer anything but delirium and madness. There is no complete system, synthesis, or cosmology that is not imaginary.[49] With the belief in the existence of bodies, fiction itself as a principle is opposed to the principles of association: the latter are *principally* instead of being *subsequently* excessive, as it is the case with general rules. Fantasy triumphs. To oppose its own nature and to allow its fancies to be deployed has become the nature of the mind. Here, the most insane is still natural.[50] The system is a mad delirium. Hume shows in the hypothesis of an independent existence the first step toward this delirium. Subsequently, he studies the manner in which independent existence is formed in ancient and modern philosophy. Ancient philosophy forges the delirium of substances, substantial forms, accidents, and occult qualities[51]—"specters in the dark."[52] But the new philosophy has also its ghosts. It thinks that it can recuperate reason by distinguishing primary from secondary qualities, but in the end it is no less mad than the other.[53] But if the mind is manifested as a *delirium*, it is because it is first of all, and essentially, *madness*.[54] As soon as extension becomes a principle, it follows its own way, and reflection follows another way: two principles which cannot destroy each other are opposed. ". . . [N]or is it possible for us to reason justly and regularly from causes and effects, and at the same time believe the continu'd existence of matter. How then shall we adjust those principles together? Which of them shall we prefer?"[55] The worst is that these two principles are mutually implicated, since belief in the existence of bodies essentially encompasses causality. But, on the other hand, the principles of association, insofar as they constitute the given as a system, generate the presentation of the given in the guise of a world. It follows that the choice is to be made not between one or the other of the two principles but rather between all or nothing, *between the contradiction or nothingness*. "We have, therefore, no choice left but betwixt a false reason and none at all."[56] And this is the state of *madness*. That is why, then, it would be vain to hope that we could separate within the mind its reason from its *delirium*, its permanent, irresistible, and universal principles, from its variable,

fanciful, and irregular principles.[57] Modern philosophy hopes, and
there lies its error. We do not have the means of choosing the understanding over the suggestions of the imagination. ". . . [T]he understanding, when it acts alone, according to its most general principles, entirely subverts itself, and leaves not the lowest degree of
evidence in any proposition, either in philosophy or common life."[58]
The function of the understanding to reflect on something is exclusively corrective; functioning alone, the understanding can do
only one thing *ad infinitum*—to correct its corrections, so that all
certainty, even practical certainty, is compromised and lost.[59]

We have seen three critical states of the mind. *Indifference and fancy*
are the situations proper to the mind, independently of the external
principles which fix it through the association of its ideas. *Madness*
is the contradiction in the mind between these principles which affect
it and the fiction which it affirms as a principle. *Delirium* is the system
of fictional reconciliations between principles and fiction. The only
resource and positivity offered to the mind is nature or practice—
moral practice and, based on the image of the latter, practice of the
understanding. Instead of referring nature to the mind, the mind
must be referred to nature. "I may, nay I must yield to the current
of nature, in submitting to my senses and understanding; and in this
blind submission I shew most perfectly my sceptical disposition and
principles."[60]

Madness is human nature related to the mind, just as good sense
is the mind related to human nature; each one is the reverse of the
other. This is the reason why we must reach the depths of madness
and solitude in order to find a passage to good sense. I could not,
without reaching contradiction, refer the affections of the mind to
the mind itself: the mind is identical to its ideas, and the affection
does not let itself be expressed through ideas without a decisive
contradiction. On the other hand, the mind related to its affections
constitutes the entire domain of general rules and beliefs. This domain is the middle and temperate region, where the contradiction
between human nature and the imagination already exists, and always
subsists, but this contradiction is regulated by possible corrections
and resolved through practice. In short, there is no science or life
except at the level of general rules and beliefs.

FIVE

EMPIRICISM
AND SUBJECTIVITY

WE THOUGHT THAT we had located the essence of empiricism in the specific problem of subjectivity. But, first of all, we should ask how subjectivity is defined. The subject is defined by the movement through which it is developed. Subject is that which develops itself. The only content that we can give to the idea of subjectivity is that of mediation and transcendence. But we note that the movement of self-development and of becoming-other is double: the subject transcends itself, but it is also reflected upon. Hume recognized these two dimensions, presenting them as the fundamental characteristics of human nature: inference and invention, belief and artifice. One should then avoid attributing too much importance to the analogy, often noted, between belief and sympathy. This is not to say that this analogy is not real. But, if it is true that belief is the knowing act of the subject, then his moral act, on the contrary, is not sympathy; it is rather artifice or invention, with respect to which sympathy, corresponding to belief, is only a necessary condition. In short, believing and inventing is what makes the subject a subject.

From what is given, I infer the existence of that which is not given: I believe. Caesar is dead, Rome did exist, the sun will rise, and bread is nourishing. At the same time and through the same operation, while transcending the given, I judge and posit myself as subject. I affirm more than I know. Therefore, the problem of truth must be presented and stated as the critical problem of subjectivity itself. By what right does man affirm more than he knows? Between the sensible qualities and the powers of nature, we infer an unknown connection:

> . . . (W)hen we see like sensible qualities that they have like secret powers, (we) expect that effects, similar to those which we have experienced, will follow from them. If a body of like colour and consistence with that bread, which we have formerly eat, be presented to us, we make no scruple of repeating the experiment, and foresee, with certainty, like nourishment and support. Now this is a process of the mind or thought, of which I would willingly know the foundation.[1]

We are also subjects in another respect, that is, in (and by) the moral, aesthetic, or social judgment. In this sense, the subject reflects and is reflected upon. It extracts from that which affects it in general a power independent of the actual exercise, that is, a pure function, and then transcends its own partiality.[2] Consequently, artifice and invention have been made possible. The subject invents; it is the maker of artifice. Such is the dual power of subjectivity: to believe and to invent, to assume the secret powers and to presuppose abstract or distinct powers. In these two senses, the subject is normative; it creates norms or general rules. We must explain and find the foundation, law, or principle of this dual power—this dual exercise of general rules. This is the problem. For nothing escapes our knowledge as radically as the powers of Nature,[3] and nothing is more futile for our understanding than the distinction between powers and their exercise.[4] How can we assume or distinguish them? To believe is to infer one part of nature from another, which is not given. To invent is to distinguish powers and to constitute functional totalities or totalities that are not given in nature.

The problem is as follows: how can a subject transcending the given be constituted in the given? Undoubtedly, the subject itself is given. Undoubtedly, that which transcends the given is also given, in another way and in another sense. This subject who invents and believes is constituted inside the given in such a way that it makes the given itself a synthesis and a system. This is what we must explain. In this formulation of the problem, we discover the absolute essence of empiricism. We could say that philosophy in general has always sought a plane of analysis in order to undertake and conduct the examination of the structures of consciousness (critique), and to justify the totality of experience. Initially, it is a difference in plan that opposes critical philosophies. We embark upon a transcendental critique when, having situated ourselves on a methodologically reduced plane that provides an essential certainty—a certainty of essence—we ask: how can there be a given, how can something be given to a subject, and how can the subject give something to itself? Here, the critical requirement is that of a constructivist logic which finds its model in mathematics. The critique is empirical when, having situated ourselves in a purely immanent point of view, which makes possible a description whose rule is found in determinable hypotheses and whose model is found in physics, we ask: how is the subject constituted in the given? The construction of the given makes room for the constitution of the subject. The given is no longer given to a subject; rather, the subject constitutes itself in the given. Hume's merit lies in the singling out of this empirical problem in its pure state and its separation from the transcendental and the psychological.

But what is the given? It is, says Hume, the flux of the sensible, a collection of impressions and images, or a set of perceptions. It is the totality of that which appears, being which equals appearance;[5] it is also movement and change without identity or law. We use the terms "*imagination*" and "*mind*" not to designate a faculty or a principle of organization, but rather a particular set or a particular collection. Empiricism begins from the experience of a collection, or from an animated succession of distinct perceptions. It begins with them, insofar as they are distinct and independent. In fact, its principle, that is, the constitutive principle giving a status to experience, is not that "every idea derives from an impression" whose sense is only regulative; but rather that "everything separable is distinguishable and everything distinguishable is different."

This is the principle of difference. "For how is it possible we can separate what is not distinguishable, or distinguish what is not different?"[6] Therefore, experience is succession, or the movement of separable ideas, insofar as they are different, and different, insofar as they are separable. We must begin with *this* experience because it is *the* experience. It does not presuppose anything else and nothing else precedes it. It is not the affection of an implicated subject, nor the modification or mode of a substance. If every discernible perception is a separate existence, "[it has] no need of any thing to support [its] existence."[7]

The mind is identical to ideas in the mind. If we wish to retain the term "substance," to find a use for it at all costs, we must apply it correctly not to a substrate of which we have no idea but to each individual perception. We would then claim that "every perception is a substance, and every distinct part of a perception a distinct substance."[8]

The mind is not a subject, nor does it require a subject whose mind it would be. Hume's entire critique, especially his critique of the principle of sufficient reason in its denunciations of sophisms and contradictions,[9] amounts to this: if the subject is indeed that which transcends the given, we should not initially attribute to the given the capacity to transcend itself.

On the other hand, the mind is not the representation of nature either. Not only are perceptions the only substances, they are also the only objects.[10] The negation of the primary qualities corresponds now to the negation of the principle of sufficient reason:[11] perception gives us no difference between two kinds of qualities. The philosophy of experience is not only the critique of a philosophy of substance but also the critique of a philosophy of nature. Therefore, ideas are not the representations of objects, but rather of impressions; as for the impressions, they are not representative, nor are they adventitious;[12] rather, they are innate.[13] Undoubtedly, there is a nature, there are real operations, and bodies do have powers. But we must restrict "our speculations to *the appearance* of objects to our senses, without entering into disquisitions concerning their real nature and operation. . . ."[14] And this skepticism is not so much a renunciation as a requirement identical to the preceding one. The two critiques, in fact, merge to the point where they become one. Why? Because the question of a determinable relation with nature has its own conditions: it is not obvious, it is not given, and it can only be posited by a subject questioning the value of the system of his judgments, that is, the legitimacy of the transformation to which he subjects the given, or the legitimacy of the organization which he attributes to it. Therefore, the real problem would be to think, at the right moment, of a harmony between the unknown powers on which the given appearances depend and the transcendent principles which determine the constitution of a subject within the given. The real problem would be to think of a harmony between the powers of nature and the subject. As for the given, in itself and as such, it is neither the representation of the first nor the modification of the second.

We might say that the given is at least given to the senses and that it presupposes organs and even a brain. This is true, but one must always avoid endowing, in the beginning, the organism with an organization, an organization that will come about only when the subject itself comes to mind, that is, an organization that depends on the same principles as the subject. Thus, in a central passage, Hume envisages a physiological explanation of association and subjectivity: ". . . upon our conception of any idea, the animal spirits run into all the contiguous traces, and rouze up the other ideas, that are related to it."[15]

Hume himself presents this explanation as "probable and plausible," but, as he says, he neglects it willingly. When he appeals to it, it is not in order to explain association, but rather, in order to account for the errors resulting from the association.[16] For if such an organization of the brain provides us with a physiological model applicable to the associative process, it nonetheless presupposes the principles upon which this model depends and for which it cannot account. In short, the organism and its senses do not immediately and in themselves have the characteristics of human nature or of a subject; they must acquire these somewhere else. The mechanism of the body cannot explain the spontaneity of the subject. By itself and in itself, an organ is merely a collection of impressions considered in the mechanism of their appearance: "External objects are seen, and felt, and become present to the mind; that is, they acquire such a relation to a connected heap of perceptions. . . ."[17] In a word, we always return to the same conclusion; the given, the mind, the collection of perceptions cannot call upon anything other than themselves.

But as it calls upon itself, what exactly is it calling upon, since the collection remains arbitrary, since every idea and every impres-

sion can disappear or be separated from the mind without contradiction?[18] How can we discuss the mind or the given in general?
What is the consistency of the mind? After all, it is not under the
category of quality that we must consider the mind as mind but
rather form the viewpoint of quantity. It is not the representative
quality of the idea but rather its divisibility that interests us at this
stage. *The fundamental principle of empiricism, the principle of difference,
had already stated this; such was its meaning.* The mind's constant is
not a particular idea, but rather the smallest idea. An idea may appear
or disappear, I can always discover others; but sometimes smaller
ideas cannot be found. "In rejecting the infinite capacity of the mind,
we suppose it may arrive at an end in the division of its ideas."[19]
What is essential in an idea is not that it represents something but
rather that it is indivisible:

> When you tell me of the thousandth and ten thousandth
> part of a grain of sand, I have a distinct idea of these numbers
> and of their different proportions; but the images, which I
> form in my mind to represent the things themselves, are
> nothing different form each other, nor inferior to that image,
> by which I represent the grain of sand itself. . . . But what-
> ever we may imagine of the thing, the idea of a grain of
> sand is not distinguishable, nor separable into twenty, much
> less into a thousand, or an infinite number of different ideas.[20]

We call "moment of the mind" the reflection that relates ideas
or impressions[21] to the criterion of division of ideas. The mind and
the given are not derived form such-and-such an idea but rather
from the smallest idea, whether it is used to represent the grain of
sand or a fraction of it. This is why, finally, the problem of the
status of the mind is the same as the problem of space. On one hand,
we ask whether or not extension is infinitely divisible. On the other
hand, the indivisible ideas, to the extent that they are indivisible,
constitute in a certain way extension. Hume presents these two theses
as the two intimately connected parts of the system.[22]

Let us consider the first part.[23] To say that the mind has a finite
capacity is to say that "the imagination reaches a *minimum*."[24] Hume
calls this minimum "unity"[25] "indivisible point,"[26] "impression of
atoms or corpuscles,"[27] "terminating idea."[28] Nothing smaller exists,

and by "nothing" we should understand not simply "no other idea," but also "no other thing in general."[29] The idea-limit is absolutely indivisible. It is in itself indivisible to the extent that it is indivisible for the mind and because it is an idea. Existence itself belongs to the unit.[30] This is why the mind possesses and manifests objectivity. Hume's entire theme reconciles the defects of the senses and the objectivity of the given as follows: undoubtedly there are many things smaller than the smallest bodies that appear to our senses; the fact is, though, that there is nothing smaller than the impression that we have of these bodies or the ideas that we form of them.[31]

As for the second part of the thesis,[32] we can see that it is determined by the first. The smallest impression is neither a mathematical nor a physical point, but rather a sensible one.[33] A physical point is already extended and divisible; a mathematical point is nothing. Between the two there is a midpoint which is the only real one. Between real extension and nonexistence there is real existence whose extension will be precisely formed. A sensible point or atom is visible and tangible, colored and solid. By itself, it has no extension, and yet it exists. It exists and we have seen why. In the possibility of its existence and in the reason for its distinct existence, empiricism discovers a principle. It is not extended, since no extension is itself an atom, a corpuscle, a minimum idea, or a simple impression. "Five notes play'd on a flute give us the impression and idea of time; tho' time be not a sixth impression, which presents itself to the hearing or any other of the senses."[34] Similarly, the idea of space is merely the idea of visible or tangible points distributed in a certain order.[35] Space is discovered in the arrangement of visible or tangible objects, just as time is discovered in the perceptible succession of changing objects.

Thus the given is not in space; the space is in the given. Space and time are in the mind. We should nonetheless note the difference between time and space, for the latter can be given through two senses only, those of sight and touch. In fact, for the idea of space to exist it is necessary that the simple impressions, or the parts of our impressions, be arranged in a way that is provided neither by the other senses[36] nor, in the case of movement, by the impressions of the muscles.[37] Extension, therefore, is only the quality of certian perceptions.[38] This is not the case with time, which is effectively presented as the quality of any set of perceptions whatsoever.[39] "For we may observe, that there is a continual succession of perceptions in our mind; so that the idea of time being forever present with us."[40]

We must then define the given by two objective characteristics: indivisibility of an element and distribution of elements; *atom and structure*. As Laporte observed, it is entirely incorrect to say that the whole, in Hume's atomism, is nothing but the sum of its parts, since the parts, considered together, are defined, rather, according to their mode of temporal, and sometimes spatial, appearance. This is an objective and spontaneous mode, by no means indebted to reflection or to construction. In fact, Hume makes this point about space in a text whose second sentence should not be forgotten: "The perception consists of parts. These parts are so situated, as to afford us the notion of distance and contiguity, of length, breadth, and thickness."[41]

We must now raise the question: what do we mean when we speak of the subject? We mean that the imagination, having been a collection, becomes now a faculty; the distributed collection becomes now a system. The given is once again taken up by a movement, and in a movement that transcends it. The mind becomes human nature. The subject invents and believes; *it is a synthesis of the mind*. We formulate three problems: what are the characteristics of the subject in the case of belief and invention? Second, by means of what principles is the subject constituted in this way? Which factors have acted in transforming the mind? Finally, what are the various stages of the synthesis that is brought about in the mind by the subject? What are the stages of the system? We begin with the first problem. Since we previously studied the mind from three points of view—in relation to itself, in relation to the organs of the senses, and in relation to time—we must now ask what becomes of these three instances when the mind itself becomes a subject.

First, in relation to time. The mind, considered from the viewpoint of the appearance of its perceptions, was essentially succession, time. To speak of the subject now is to speak of duration, custom, habit, and anticipation. Anticipation is habit, and habit is anticipation: these two determinations—the thrust of the past and the élan toward the future—are, at the center of Hume's philosophy, the two aspects of the same fundamental dynamism. It is not necessary to force the texts in order to find in the habit-anticipation most of the characteristics of the Bergsonian *durée* or memory. Habit is the constitutive root of the subject, and the subject, at root, is the synthesis of time—the synthesis of the present and the past in light of the future. Hume demonstrates this clearly when he studies the two operations of subjectivity, namely, belief and invention. We know what is involved in invention; each subject reflects upon itself, that is, transcends its immediate partiality and avidity, by instituting rules of property which are institutions making possible an agreement among subjects. But what is it, in the nature of the subject, that grounds this mediate agreement and these general rules?

Here, Hume returns to a simple juridical theory which will also be developed by the majority of the utilitarians: each man *expects* to conserve what he already possesses.[42] The principle of frustrated anticipation will play the role of the principle of contradiction in the logic of property, that is, the role of a principle of synthetic contradiction. We know that, for Hume, there are many states of possession which are determined through complex relations: actual possession before the establishment of society; occupation, prescription, accession, and succession, after the establishment of society. Yet only the dynamism of habit and anticipation transforms these states into titles of property. Hume's originality lies in the theory of this dynamism. Anticipation is the synthesis of past and present brought about by habit. Anticipation, or the future, is the synthesis of time constituted by the subject inside the mind.

> Such is the effect of custom, that it not only reconciles us
> to anything we have long enjoy'd, but even gives us an af-
> fection for it, and makes us prefer it to other objects, which
> may be more valuable, but are less known to us.[43]

Prescription is the privileged example in this respect. In this case, it is not merely through a synthesis of time that the subject transforms the state of possession into a title of property but rather the state of possession is itself time and nothing else.

> But as 'tis certain, that, however every thing be produc'd in
> time, there is nothing real, that is produc'd by time; it fol-
> lows, that property being produc'd by time, is not any thing
> real in the objects, but is the offspring of the sentiments, on
> which alone time is found to have any influence.[44]

This is the most effective way to say that time and subject are in such a relation with respect to each other that the subject presents the synthesis of time, and that only this synthesis is productive, creative, and *inventive*.

The same applies to belief. We know that belief is only a vivid idea connected, by means of a causal relation, to a present impression.[45] Belief is a feeling or a particular way of sensing ideas.[46] Belief is the idea—the vivid idea—which is "felt rather than conceived."[47] Therefore, if we wish to analyze this feeling, we must first investigate the causal relation, since the latter communicates the vividness of the present impression to the idea. In this analysis, feeling reveals its source: once more, it is manifested as the result of the synthesis of time. Indeed, what is the causal relation in its essence? It is "... that propensity, which custom produces, to pass from an object to the idea of its usual attendant."[48] We rediscover, therefore, this dynamic unity of habit and tendency, this synthesis of a past and a present which constitutes the future, and this synthetic identity of a past experience and of an adaptation to the present.[49]

> Custom, then is the great guide of human life. ... Without the influence of custom ... we should never know how to adjust means to ends, or to employ our natural powers in the production of any effect. There would be an end at once of all action, as well as the chief part of speculation.[50]

In short, the synthesis posits the past as a *rule* for the future.[51] With respect to belief, as with property, we always encounter the same transformation: time was *the structure* of the mind, now the subject is presented as *the synthesis* of time. In order to understand the meaning of this transformation, we must note that the mind includes memory in Hume's sense of the term: we distinguish in the collection of perceptions sense impressions, ideas of memory, and ideas of imagination, according to their degrees of vividness.[52] Memory is the reappearance of an impression in the form of an idea that is still vivid. But, in fact, memory alone does not bring about a synthesis of time; it does not transcend the structure, its essential role becomes the reproduction of the different structures of the given.[53] It is rather habit which presents itself as a synthesis, and habit belongs to the subject. Recollection is the old present, not the past. We should call "past" not only that which has been, but also that which determines, acts, prompts, and carries a certain weight. In this sense, not only is habit to memory what the subject is to the mind, but also habit easily does without this dimension of the mind which we call "memory"; habit has no need of memory, it does without it ordinarily, in one way or another. Sometimes no evocation of memories accompanies it,[54] and sometimes, there is no specific memory that it could evoke.[55] In a word, the past as such is not given. It is constituted through, and in, a synthesis which gives the subject its real origin and its source.

We are thus led to specify how we must understand this synthesis of past and present, for this is not clear. Obviously, *if we give ready made the past and the present to ourselves*, the synthesis is made on its own; it is already formed and, therefore, no longer a problem. Also, since the future is constituted through this synthesis of the past and the present, it is no longer a problem either under these conditions. Thus, when Hume says that the most difficult thing is to explain how we are able to constitute the past as a rule for the future, it is not easy to see where the difficulty lies. Hume himself feels the need to convince us that he is not trying to create paradoxes.[56]

> In vain do you pretend to have learned the nature of bodies from your past experience. Their secret nature, and consequently all their effects and influence, may change, without any change in their sensible qualities. This happens sometimes, and with regard to some objects: Why may it not happen always, and with regard to all subjects? What logic, what process of argument secures you against this supposition? *My practice, you say, refutes my doubts. But you mistake the purport of my question. As an agent, I am quite satisfied in the point; but as a philosopher, who has some share of curiosity, I will not say sceptism, I want to learn the foundation of this inference.*[57]

In practice, there is no problem, for, once the past and the present are given, the synthesis is given at the same time. But, in fact, the problem is elsewhere. Present and past, the former understood as the starting point of an élan and the latter as the object of an observation, are not characteristics of time. It would be better to say that they are the products of the synthesis rather than its constitutive elements. But even this would not be exact. The truth of the matter is that past and present are constituted within time, under the influence of certain principles, and that the synthesis of time itself is nothing but this constitution, organization, and double affection. This then is the problem: how are a present and a past constituted *within time*? Viewed from this angle, the analysis of the causal relation in its essential duality acquires its full meaning. On one hand, Hume presents *experience* as a principle which manifests a multiplicity and a repetition of similar cases; literally, this principle affects the span of the past. On the other hand, he finds in habit another principle inciting us to move from one object to a second which follows it— a principle which organizes time as a perpetual present to which we can, and must, adapt.

Now, if we consult the distinctions established by Hume in his analysis of "the inference from the impression to the idea,"[58] we could offer a number of definitions. The understanding is the mind itself which, under the influence of experience, reflects time in the form of a past entity subject to its observation. The imagination, under the influence of the principle of habit, is also the mind which reflects time as a determined future filled with its anticipation. Belief is the relation between these two constituted dimensions. As he gives the formula of belief, Hume writes: "[the two principles conspiring] to operate upon the imagination, make me form certain ideas in a more intense and lively manner, than others, which are not attended with the same advantages."[59]

We have just seen how time is transformed when the subject is constituted in the mind. We can now move on to the second point: what happens to the organism? Earlier, the organism was presented as the mechanism only of distinct perceptions. Now, to say that the subject is constituted in the mind amounts to saying that, under the influence of principles, the organism takes on a dual spontaneity. First, it takes on a *spontaneity of relation*.[60] ". . . [U]pon our conception of any idea, the animal spirits run into all the contiguous traces and rouze up the other ideas, that are related to it."[61] We have already said that for the animal spirits to find, in the *neighboring* traces into which they fall, ideas which are *tied* to the one that the mind wanted to see, it is, first, necessary that the ideas themselves be associated in the mind. It is necessary that the mechanism of distinct perceptions be divided again, in a certain way, within the body itself through a physical spontaneity of relations—a spontaneity of the body that depends on the same principles as subjectivity. Earlier, the body was merely the mind, that is, the collection of ideas and impressions envisaged from the point of view of the mechanism of their distinct production. Now, the body is the subject itself envisaged from the viewpoint of the spontaneity of the relations that, under the influence of principles, it establishes between ideas.

On the other hand, there is a *spontaneity of disposition.* We have seen the importance that Hume places on the distinction between two kinds of impressions, namely, those of sensation and those of reflection. Our entire problem depends on this, since the impressions of sensation only form the mind, giving it merely an origin, whereas the impressions of reflection constitute the subject in the mind, diversely qualifying the mind as subject. Undoubtedly, Hume presents these impressions of reflection as being part of the collection, but, *first of all*, they must be formed. In their formation, they depend on a particular process and on principles of subjectivity. ". . . [N]or can the mind, by revolving over a thousand times all its ideas of sensation, ever extract from them any new original idea, *unless nature has so fram'd its faculties, that it feels some new original impression arise from such a contemplation.*"[62]

The problem, thus, is knowing which new dimension the principles of subjectivity confer upon the body when they constitute impressions of reflection in the mind. The impressions of sensation were defined by means of a mechanism, and referred to the body as a procedure of this mechanism. The impressions of reflection are defined by means of a spontaneity or a disposition and are referred to the body as the biological source of this spontaneity. As he studies the passions, Hume analyzes this new dimension of the body. The organism is disposed to produce passions. It has a disposition which is proper and specific to the passion in question, as an "original, internal movement."[63] This is the case with hunger, thirst, and sexual desire.[64] One could object, nonetheless, that not all passions are like these. There are passions, such as pride and humility, love and hatred, love between the sexes, joy and sadness, to which no *specific* bodily disposition corresponds. In this case, nature does not produce passions "by itself immediately," but "must be assisted by the co-operation of other causes."[65] These causes are natural, yet not original.[66] Here, in other words, the role of the bodily disposition is only taken up by an external object which will produce passions in natural and determinable circumstances. This means that, even in this case, we can understand the phenomenon of the passions only through the corporeal disposition: "As nature has given to the body certain appetites and inclinations . . . she has proceeded in the same manner with the mind."[67] But what is the meaning of disposition? Through the mediation of the passions, disposition spontaneously incites the appearance of an idea, namely, an idea of the object corresponding to the passion.[68]

We are left with the last, and more general, point of view: without any other criterion, we must compare the subject with the mind. But because this point is the most general, it already leads to the second problem, mentioned earlier: what are the principles constituting the subject in the mind? What factors will transform the mind? We have seen that Hume's answer is simple: what transforms the mind into a subject and constitutes the subject in the mind are the principles of human nature. These principles are of two kinds: *principles of association* and principles of the passions, which, in some respects, we could present in the general form of the principle of utility. The subject is the entity which, under the influence of the principle of utility, pursues a goal or an intention; it organizes means in view of an end and, under the influence of the principles of association, establishes relations among ideas. Thus, the collection becomes a system. The collection of perceptions, when organized and bound, becomes a system.

Let us examine the problem of relations. We should not debate futile points; we do not have to ask: on the assumption that relations do not depend upon ideas, is it *eo ipso* certain that they depend on the subject? This is obvious. If relations do not have as their causes the properties of the ideas between which they are established, that is, if they have other causes, then these other causes determine a subject which alone establishes relations. The relation of truth to subjectivity is manifested in the affirmation that a true judgment is not a tautology. Thus, the truly fundamental proposition is that relations are external to ideas. And if they are external, the problem of the subject, as it is formulated in empiricism, follows. It is necessary, in fact, to know upon what other causes these relations depend, *that is, how the subject is constituted in the collection of ideas.* Relations are external to their terms. When James calls himself a pluralist, he does not say, in principle, anything else. This is also the case when Russell calls himself a realist. We see in this statement the point common to all empiricisms.

It is true that Hume distinguishes between two kinds of relations: "such as may be chang'd without any change in the ideas" (identity, temporal and spatial relations, causality), and those that "depend entirely on the ideas which we compare together" (resemblance, contrariety, degrees of quality, and propositions of quantity and number).[69] It seems that the latter are not, in this sense, external to ideas. And this is exactly what Kant believed, when he criticized Hume for taking mathematics to be a system of analytic judgments. But it is nothing of the sort. Every relation is external to its terms. ". . . [L]et us consider, that since equality is a relation, it is not, strictly speaking, a property in the figures themselves, but arises merely from the comparison, which the mind makes betwixt them."[70]

We have seen that the ideas can be considered in two ways, collectively and individually, distributively and singly, in the determinable collection where their own modes of appearance place them, and in their own characteristics. This is the origin of the distinction between the two kinds of relations. But both are equally external to the ideas. Let us examine the first kind. Spatial and temporal relations (distance, contiguity, anteriority, posteriority, etc.) give us, in diverse forms, the relation of a variable object with the totality within which it is integrated, or with the structure where its mode of appearance situates it. One might say, though, that the mind as such already provided us with the notions of distance and contiguity.[71] This is true, but it was merely giving us a matter—not actual principles—to confront. Contiguous or distant objects do not in the least explain that distance and contiguity are *relations.* In the mind, space and time were only a *composition.* Under which influence (external to the mind, since the mind undergoes it as they do, and finds in its constraint a constancy which it itself does not possess) do they become a relation?

The originality of the relation appears even more clearly in the problem of identity. In fact, the relation here is a *fiction.* We apply the idea of time to an invariable object, and we compare the representation of the immutable object with the sequence of our perceptions.[72] And even more clearly we know that in the case of causality the relation is *transcendence*.[73] If, now, the relations of the second kind tend to be more confusing, it is because this second kind relates only the characteristics of two or more ideas being considered individually. Resemblance, in the narrow sense of the term, compares qualities; proportions compare quantities; the degrees of quality compare intensities. We should not be surprised that, in this case, the relations cannot change without [there being] a change in the ideas. In fact, what is being considered, what gives the comparison its subject matter is a specific, objectively discernible idea and not a particular collection, effectively determinable but always arbitrary. These relations are no less external. The resemblance between particular ideas does not explain that resemblance is a relation, that is, that an idea can evoke the appearance of a similar idea in the mind. The indivisibility of ideas does not explain that the unities constituted by them can be added, subtracted, made equal, or that they can enter into a system of *operations*. Nor does it explain that the lengths which they compose, in virtue of their arrangement, can be *measured* and *evaluated*. Here, we recognize the two distinct problems of arithmetic and geometry. The relation always presupposes a synthesis, and neither the idea nor the mind can account for it. The relation, in a way, designates "that particular circumstance, in which ... we may think proper to compare [two ideas]."[74] "To think proper" is the best expression; it is, in fact, a normative expression. The problem is to find the norms of this judgment, of this decision, and the norms of subjectivity. In the last analysis, we will have to speak about Hume's voluntarism, but then the problem would be to show the principles of this will which are independent of the characteristics of the mind.

These principles are, *first of all*, those of association: contiguity, resemblance, and causality. Evidently these notions should be given a meaning different from the ones given earlier, when they were presented only as examples of relations. Relations are the *effect* of the principles of association. These principles naturalize and give constancy to the mind. It seems that each of them is specifically addressed to one aspect of the mind: contiguity, to the senses; causality, to time; resemblance, to imagination.[75] Their common point is the designation of a quality that leads the mind *naturally* from one idea to another.[76] We already know the meaning that we must give to the term "quality." That an idea naturally introduces another is not a quality of the idea, but rather a quality of human nature. Only human nature is qualificatory. A collection of ideas will never explain how the same simple ideas are regularly grouped into complex ideas. Ideas, "most suited to be united in a complex idea," must be *designated* to each one of us. These ideas are not designated within the mind without the mind becoming subject—a subject *to whom* these ideas are designated, a subject who *speaks*. Ideas are designated in the mind at the same time that the mind itself becomes a subject. In short, the effects of the principle of association are complex ideas: relations, substances and modes, general ideas. Under the influence of the principles of association, ideas are compared, grouped, and evoked. This relation, or rather this intimacy, between complex ideas and the subject, such that one is the inverse of the others, is presented to us in language; the subject, as she speaks, designates in some way ideas which are in turn designated to her.

Relations are external to their terms. This means that ideas do not account for the nature of the operations that we perform on them, and especially of the relations that we establish among them. The principles of human nature, or the principles of association, are the necessary conditions of relations. But has the problem been resolved? When Hume defines the relation as "this particular circumstance for the sake of which we think proper to compare two ideas," he adds: "even when the latter are arbitrarily linked in the imagination"—that is, even when the one does not naturally introduce the other. In fact, association is insufficient to explain relations. Undoubtedly, it alone makes them possible. Undoubtedly, it accounts entirely for immediate or direct relations, that is, those that are established between two ideas without the intervention of another idea of the collection. For example, it explains the relation between two, immediately adjacent shades of blue, or between two contiguous objects, etc. Let us say that it explains that A=B and B=C; but it does not explain that A=C or that distance itself is a relation.[77] Later, we will see that Hume calls that which the association explains a "natural relation," and that which it does not suffice to explain a "philosophical relation." He insists heavily on this point: the characteristic of nature is to be natural, easy going, and immediate. In meditations, it loses its force and vividness, that is, its effect. Intermediaries exhaust it and, to each one, it loses something of itself:

Where the mind reaches not its objects with easiness and facility, the same principles have not the same effect as in a more natural conception of the ideas; nor does the imagination feel a sensation, which holds any proportion with that which arises from its common judgments and opinions.[78]

How can the mediations (or the relations that are established between the most remote objects) be justified? Resemblance, Hume claims, does not always produce "a connexion or association of ideas. *When a quality becomes very general, and is common to a great many individuals, it leads not the mind directly to anyone of them; but by presenting at once too great a choice, does thereby prevent the imagination from fixing on any single object.*"[79]

Most of the objections raised against associationism amount to this: the principles of association explain, at best, the form of thinking in general and not its particular contents. Association explains only the surface or "the crust" of our consciousness. Writers as different as Bergson and Freud converge on this point. Bergson, in a famous passage, writes:

For we should seek in vain for two ideas which have not some point of resemblance, or which do not touch each other somewhere. To take similarity first: however profound are the differences which separate two images, we shall always find, if we go back high enough, a common genus to which they belong, and consequently a resemblance which may serve as a connecting link between them. . . . This is as much as to say that between any two ideas chosen at random there is always a resemblance, and always, even, contiguity; so that when we discover a relation of contiguity or of resemblance between two successive ideas, we have in no way explained why the one evokes the other. What we really need to discover is how a choice is affected among an infinite number of recollections which all resemble in some way the present perception, and why only one of them—this rather than that—emerges into the light of consciousness.[80]

The least that we can say is that Hume thought of it first. In his work, the association of ideas accounts effectively for *habits of thought, everyday notions of good sense, current ideas, and complexes of ideas which correspond to the most general and most constant needs common to all minds and all languages.*[81] What it does not account for is the difference between one mind and another. The specific progress of a mind must be studied, and there is an entire casuistry to be worked out: why does this perception evoke a specific idea, rather than another, in a particular consciousness at a particular moment? The association of ideas does not explain that this idea has been evoked instead of another. It follows that, from this point of view, we must define relation as "... that *particular* circumstance, in which, *even upon the arbitrary union of two ideas in the fancy,* we may think proper to compare them."[82] If it is true that association is necessary in order to make all relations in general possible, each particular relation is not in the least explained by the association. *Circumstance* gives the relation its sufficient reason.

The notion "circumstance" appears constantly in Hume's philosophy. It is at the center of history and it makes possible a science of the particular and a differential psychology. When Freud and Bergson demonstrate that the association of ideas explains only that which is superficial in us, that is, only the formalism of consciousness, they mean, essentially, that only affectivity can justify the singular content, the profound and the particular. And they are right. But Hume has never said anything else. He merely thought that the superficial and the formal *should also be explained,* and that this task was, in a sense, the most important. And for the rest, he appeals to circumstance. This notion, for him, always refers to affectivity. We must take literally the idea that affectivity is a matter of circumstances. These are precisely the variables that define our passions and our interests. Understood in this way, a set of circumstances always individuates a subject since it represents a state of its passions and needs, an allocation of its interests, a distribution of its beliefs and exhilarations.[83] As a result, we see that the principles of the passions must be combined with the principles of association in order for the subject to constitute itself within the mind. If the principles of association explain that ideas are associated, only the principles of the passions can explain that a particular idea, rather than another, is associated at a given moment.

Circumstances are not only required by relations; they are also required by substances and modes, as well as by general ideas.

> As the individuals are collected together, and plac'd under
> a general term with a view to that resemblance, which they
> bear to each other, this relation must facilitate their entrance
> in the imagination, and make them be suggested more read-
> ily upon occasion. . . . Nothing is more admirable, than the
> readiness, with which the imagination suggests its ideas, and
> presents them *at the very instant, in which they become necessary
> or useful.*[84]

We see that, in all cases, the subject is presented in the mind under the influence of two kinds of combined principles. Everything takes place as if the principles of association provided the subject with its necessary form, whereas the principles of the passions provided it with its singular content. The latter function as the principle for the individuation of the subject. This duality, however, does not signify an opposition between the singular and the universal. The principles of the passions are no less universal or constant than the others. They define laws in which circumstances only act as variables. They do indeed involve the individual, but only in the precise sense in which a science of the individual can be, and is, developed. We must then ask, in the third and last problem that remains to be solved, what is the difference between, and unity of, these two kinds of principles—a unity that must be followed and disengaged from every step of this combined action. Yet, we can already, at least, foresee how this unity will manifest itself within the subject. If the relation cannot be separated from the circumstances, if the subject cannot be separated from the singular content which is strictly essential to it, it is because subjectivity is essentially *practical*. Its definitive unity— that is, the unity of relations and circumstances—will be revealed in the relations between motive and action, means and end. *These relations, means-end, motive-action, are indeed relations, but they are also something more.* The fact that there is no theoretical subjectivity, and that there cannot be one, becomes the fundamental claim of empiricism. And, if we examine it closely, it is merely another way of saying that the subject is constituted within the given. If the subject is constituted within the given, then, in fact, there is only a practical subject.

SIX

PRINCIPLES OF
HUMAN NATURE

ATOMISM IS THE theory of ideas, insofar as relations are external to them. Associationism is the theory of relations, insofar as relations are external to ideas, in other words, insofar as they depend on other causes. Now, in both cases, we have seen how much we must distrust the objections often raised against Hume's empiricism. We shouldn't, of course, present Hume as an exceptional victim, who more than others has felt the unfairness of constant criticisms. The case is similar for all great philosophers. We are surprised by the objections constantly raised against Descartes, Kant, Hegel, etc. Let us say that philosophical objections are of two kinds. Most are philosophical in name only, to the extent that they are criticisms of the theory without any consideration of the nature of the problem to which the theory is responding, or the problem which provides the theory with its foundation and structure. Thus Hume is reproached for the "atomization" of the given. Critics believe that an entire system can be adequately denounced by showing its basis in Hume's personal views, a particular taste of his own, or the spirit of his time. What a philosopher *says* is offered as if it were what he *does* or as what he *wants*. We are presented with a fictitious psychology of the intentions of the theorist, as if it were a sufficient criticism of the theory. Atomism and associationism are therefore treated as shifty projects which disqualify, *ab initio*, those who form them. "Hume has pulverized the given." But what does one think has been explained by this? Does one believe something important has been said? We must understand what a philosophical theory is, the basis of its concept, for it is not born from itself or for the fun of it. It is not even enough to say that it is a response to a set of problems. Undoubtedly, this explanation has the advantage, at least, of locating the necessity for a theory in a relation to something that can serve as its foundation; but this relation would be scientific rather than philosophical. In fact, a philosophical theory is an elaborately developed question, and nothing else; by itself and in itself, it is not the resolution to a problem, but the elaboration, *to the very end*, of the necessary implications of a formulated question. It shows us what things are, or what things should be, on the assumption that the question is good and rigorous. To put something in question means subordinating and subjecting things to the question, intending, through this constrained and forced subsumption, that they reveal an essence or a nature. To criticize the question means showing under what conditions the question is possible and correctly raised; in other words, how things would not be what they are were the question different from the one formulated. This means that these two operations are one and the same; the question is always about the necessary development of the implications of a problem and about giving sense to philosophy as theory. In philosophy, the question and the critique of the question are one; or, if you wish, there is no critique of solutions, there are only critiques of problems. For example, in the case of Descartes, the doubt is problematic not simply because it is provisional but rather because the doubt is the statement—pushed to the limit—of the conditions of the problem to which the *cogito* responds or, rather, of the question whose first implications the *cogito* develops. In this sense, we can see that most of the objections raised against the great philosophers are empty. People say to them: things are not like that. But, in fact, it is not a matter of knowing whether things are like that or not; it is a matter of knowing *whether the question which presents things in such a light is good or not, rigorous or not*. Hume is told that the given is not a group of atoms and that association cannot explain the singular content of a thought. The reader should not be surprised to find in the text itself the literal refutation of all these objections—despite the fact that the objections come after the text.

In truth, only one kind of objection is worthwhile: the objection which shows that the question raised by a philosopher is not a good question, that it does not force the nature of things enough, that it should be raised in another way, that we should raise it in a better way, or that we should raise a different question. It is exactly in this way that a great philosopher objects to another: for example, as we will see later, this is how Kant criticizes Hume. Certainly, we know that a philosophical theory involves psychological and, above all, sociological factors. But again, these factors are relevant only to the question and to nothing else. They are relevant only to the extent that they give it a motivation; they do not tell us whether or not it is a true or a false question. It follows that we cannot raise against Hume any objections we wish. It is not a matter of saying: he pulverized and atomized the given. It is only a matter of knowing whether the question he raises is the most rigorous possible. Hume posits the question of the subject and situates it in the following terms: *the subject is constituted inside the given.* He presents the conditions of possibilities and the criticism of the question in the following way: *relations are external to ideas.* As for atomism and associationism, these are but the implications developed from *this* question. If we want to object, it is this question that we must assess, and nothing else: really, there is nothing else.

We need not attempt this assessment here; it belongs to philosophy, and not to the history of philosophy. It is sufficient for us to know that empiricism is definable, that it defines itself only through the position of a precise problem, and through the presentation of the conditions of this problem. No other definition is possible. The classical definition of empiricism proposed by the Kantian tradition is this: empiricism is the theory according to which knowledge not only begins with experience but is derived from it. But *why* would the empiricist say that? and as the result of which question? This definition, to be sure, has at least the advantage of avoiding a piece of nonsense: were empiricism to be presented simply as a theory according to which knowledge begins only with experience, there would not have been any philosophy or philosophers—Plato and Leibniz included—who would not be empiricists. The fact is, though, that the definition is in no way satisfactory: first of all, because knowledge is not the most important thing for empiricism, but only the means to some practical activity. Next, because experience for the empiricist, and for Hume in particular, does not have this univocal and constitutive aspect that we give it. Experience has two senses, which are rigorously defined by Hume, and in neither of these senses is it constitutive. According to the first, if we call "experience" a collection of distinct perceptions, we should then recognize that relations are not derived from experience. They are the effect of the principles of association, namely of the principles of human nature, which, within experience, constitute a subject capable of transcending experience. And if we use the word in the second sense, in order to denote various conjunctions of past objects, we should again recognize that principles do not come from experience, since, on the contrary, experience itself must be understood as a principle.[1]

> To consider the matter aright, reason is nothing but a wonderful and intelligible instinct in our souls, which carries us along a certain train of ideas, and endows them with particular qualities, according to their particular situations and relations. This instinct, 'tis true, arises from past observations and experience; *but can any one give the ultimate reason, why past experience and observations produces such an effect, any more than why nature alone shou'd produce it? Nature may certainly produce whatever can arise from habit: Nay, habit is nothing but one of the principles of nature, and derives all its force from that origin.*[2]

We see why Hume never showed any interest in the problems of genesis or in purely psychological problems. Relations are not the product of a genesis, but rather the effect of principles. Genesis must refer to the principles, it is merely the particular character of a principle. Empiricism is not geneticism: as much as any other philosophy, it is opposed to psychologism.

In short, it seems impossible to define empiricism as a theory according to which knowledge derives from experience. Perhaps the term "given" is better suited. But the "given" also has two meanings: the collection of ideas and experience are given; but in this collection the subject which transcends experience and the relations which do not depend on ideas are also given. This means that empiricism will not be correctly defined except by means of a dualism. Such an empirical dualism exists between terms and relations, or more exactly between the causes of perceptions and the causes of relations, between the hidden powers of nature and the principles of human nature. Only this dualism, considered under all its possible forms, can define empiricism and present it in the following fundamental question: When is the given the product of the powers of nature and when is the subject the product of the principles of human nature? "How is the subject constituted inside the given?" A school can legitimately call itself empiricist only if it develops at least some form of this duality. Often, modern schools of logic legitimately call themselves empiricist, because they begin with the duality of relations and terms. The same duality manifests itself under the most diverse forms between relations and terms, the subject and the given, the principles of human nature and the powers of nature. Consequently, the criterion of empiricism becomes evident. We will call "nonempiricist" every theory according to which, *in one way or another*, relations are derived from the nature of things.

This relation between nature and human nature, between the powers that are at the origin of the given and the principles that constitute a subject within the given, must be thought of as an accord, for the accord is a fact. The problem of this accord provides empiricism with a real metaphysics, that is, with the problem of purposiveness: what kind of accord is there between the collection of ideas and the association of ideas, between the rule of nature and the rule of representations, between the rule of the reproduction of natural phenomena and the rule of the reproduction of mental representations? We say that Kant understood the essence of associationism, because he understood associationism from the vantage point of this problem, and he criticized it from the vantage point of the conditions of this problem. Here is the text in which Kant admirably develops his critique:

> It is a merely empirical law, that representations which have often followed or accompanied one another finally become associated, and so are set in a relation whereby, even in the absence of the object, one of these representations can, in accordance with a fixed rule, bring about a transition of the mind to the other. But this law of reproduction presupposes that appearances are themselves actually subject to such a

rule, and that in the manifold of these representations a coexistence or sequence takes place in conformity with certain rules. Otherwise our empirical imagination would never find opportunity for exercise appropriate to its powers, and so would remain concealed within the mind as a dead and to us unknown faculty. If cinnabar were sometimes red, sometimes black, sometimes light, sometimes heavy . . . my empirical imagination would never find opportunity when representing red colour to bring to mind heavy cinnabar. Nor could there be an empirical synthesis of reproduction, if a certain name were sometimes given to this, sometimes to that object, or were one and the same thing named sometimes in one way, sometimes in another, independently of any rule to which appearances are in themselves subject.

There must then be something which, as the *a priori* ground of a necessary synthetic unity of appearances, makes their reproduction possible. . . . For if we can show that even our purest *a priori* intuitions yield no knowledge, save in so far as they contain a combination of the manifold such as renders a thoroughgoing synthesis of reproduction possible, then this synthesis of imagination is likewise grounded, antecedently to all experience, upon *a priori* principles, and we must assume a pure transcendental synthesis of imagination as conditioning the very possibility of all experience. For experience as such necessarily presupposes the reproducibility of appearances.[3]

The primary interest of this text is in the fact that it situates the problem where it should be and in the way it should be, that is, on the level of the imagination. In fact, empiricism is a philosophy of the imagination and not a philosophy of the senses. We know that the question "how does the subject constitute itself within the given?" means "how does the imagination become a faculty?" According to Hume, the imagination becomes a faculty insofar as a law of the reproduction of representations or a synthesis of reproduction is constituted as the result of principles. Where does Kant's critique begin? Kant, of course, does not doubt that the imagination is effectively the best possible terrain for raising the problem of knowledge. Of the three syntheses that he distinguishes, he himself presents the synthesis of the imagination as the foundation of the other two. But Kant reproaches Hume for having mistakenly raised the problem on this good terrain: the very way in which Hume posed the question, that is, his dualism, necessitated the notion that the relation between the given and the subject is an agreement between the subject and the given, of human nature and nature. But precisely, let us suppose that the given is not *initially* subject to principles of the same kind as those that regulate the connection of representations in the case of an empirical subject. In this case, the subject could never encounter *this* agreement, except in an absolutely accidental way. It would not even have the occasion to connect its representations according to the rules whose corresponding faculty it nevertheless possessed.[4] As far as Kant is concerned, the problem must be reversed. We must relate the given to the subject, conceive the agreement as an agreement of the given with the subject, and of nature with the nature of reasonable beings. Why? Because the given is not a thing in itself, but rather a set of phenomena, a set that can be presented as a nature only by means of an *a priori* synthesis. The latter renders possible a rule of representations within the empirical imagination only on the condition that it first constitutes a rule of phenomena within nature itself. Thus, for Kant, relations depend on the nature of things in the sense that, as phenomena, things presuppose a synthesis whose source is the same as the source of relations. This is why criticial philosophy is not an empiricism. The implications of the problem reversed in this way are as follows: there is an *a priori*, that is, we must recognize a productive imagination and a transcendental activity.[5] Transcendence is an empirical fact; the transcendental is what makes transcendence immanent to something = x.[6] Another way of saying the same thing is this: *something within thought transcends (dépassera) the imagination without being able to do without it (s'en passer)*: the *a priori* synthesis of the imagination sends us over to the synthetic unity of apperception which encompasses it.[7]

Let us return, then, to the question that Hume raised in the way he raised it, which we can now better understand: how can it be developed? According to Hume, and also Kant, the principles of knowledge are not derived from experience. But in the case of Hume, nothing within thought surpasses the imagination, nothing is transcendental, because these principles are simply principles of *our* nature, and because they render possible an experience without at the same time rendering necessary the objects of this experience. Only one device will permit Hume to present the agreement between human nature and nature as something more than an accidental, indeterminate, and contingent agreement: this device will be purposiveness.

Purposiveness, that is the agreement of the subject with the given, with the powers of the given, and with nature, presents itself to us under so many different expressions, because each of these expressions corresponds to a moment, a step, or a dimension of the subject. The practical problem of a link between the various moments of subjectivity must precede the affirmation of purposiveness because this link conditions it. We must then recapitulate the moments of the general action of the principles in the mind and, for each one of these moments, we must seek the unity between the principles of association and the principles of passion. This unity confers upon the subject its successive structures. The subject must be compared to the resonance and to the increasingly louder reverberation of principles within the depths of the mind.

> Now if we consider the human mind, we shall find, that with regard to the passions, 'tis not of the nature of a wind-instrument of music, which in running over all the notes immediately loses the sound after the breath ceases; but rather resembles a string-instrument, where after each stroke the vibrations still retain some sound, which gradually and insensibly decays.[8]

What we must bring to light first of all is that the subject, being the effect of the principles within the mind, is but the mind being *activated*. We do not, then, have to ask whether for Hume the subject is active or passive, for this is a false alternative. If we did embrace it, we would have to insist on the passivity rather than the activity of the subject, since the latter is the effect of principles. The subject is the mind activated by principles, and the notion of activation avoids the alternative. To the extent that principles sink their effect into the depths of the mind, the subject, which is this very effect, becomes more and more active and less and less passive. It was passive in the beginning, it is active in the end. This confirms the idea that subjectivity is in fact a process, and that an inventory must be made of the diverse moments of this process. To speak like Bergson, let us say that the subject is an imprint, or an impression, left by principles, that it progressively turns into a machine capable of using this impression.

We must start from the pure impression and begin with principles. Principles, Hume says, act inside the mind. But what is their action? The answer is unambiguous: the effect of the principle is always an impression of reflection. Subjectivity is then an impression of reflection and nothing else. However, when Hume defines the impression of reflection, he tells us that it *proceeds* from *certain* impressions of sensation.[9] But it is precisely this proceeding or this process that the impressions of sensation are incapable of explaining: *they cannot even explain why, in the collection, they themselves are elected among others and instead of others.* "Certain" impressions of sensation are called upon to be that from which impressions of reflection proceed—but what is it that does the calling? For example, for contiguous or similar impressions to be elected, resemblance and contiguity must already be principles. For impressions of reflection to proceed from certain impressions of sensation, the mind must possess faculties constituted in an appropriate way; there must be a constitution which does not depend upon the mind—a nature.[10] Thus, the principle inserts itself between the mind and the subject, between *some* impressions of sensation and *the* impressions of reflection, making the latter proceed from the former. It is the rule of the process, the constitutive element of the constitution of the subject within the mind, the principle of its nature. We can in fact see that there are two ways of defining the principle: within the collection, the principle elects, chooses, designates, and invites certain impressions of sensation among others; having done this, it constitutes impressions of reflection in connection with these elected impressions. Thus, it has two roles at the same time: a selective role and a constitutive role. According to the first role, the principles of passion are those that choose the impressions of pleasure and pain.[11] The principles of association, on the other hand, choose the perceptions that must be brought together into a composite.[12] As they determine the process of the impressions of reflection, the principles do not develop the virtualities that would have been present in the impressions of sensation;

in fact, the latter do not contain any virtualities. The principles themselves produce and bring about the impressions of reflection; however, they bring them about in a way that causes them to begin relations with *certain* impressions of sensation.

Thus, the role of principles in general is both to designate impressions of sensation and, based upon them, to produce an impression of reflection. What is the list of principles? Being the laws of human nature and making possible a science of man, they are inevitably few in number.[13] In any case, we do not have to justify their exact number or their particular nature. Even Kant did not explain in more detail the number and the kind of categories. In a word, their list presents us with a fact. Let us begin then with the principles of association. Hume distinguishes three: contiguity, resemblance, and causality. Association has, *first of all*, three effects: general ideas, substances, and natural relations. In these three cases, the effect is an impression of reflection, a passion, a calm passion, or a determination undergone by the mind—in other words, what Hume calls a tendency, custom, freedom, or disposition. The principle constitutes this impression of reflection, in the mind, as an impression derived from impressions of sensation. This is indeed the case with general ideas: the principle of resemblance designates certain ideas that are similar, and makes it possible to group them together under the same name. Based on this name and in conjunction with a certain idea taken from the group—for example, a particular idea awakened by the name—the principle produces a habit, a strength, and a power to evoke any other particular idea of the same group; it produces an impression of reflection.[14] In the case of substances, the principles of contiguity and causality again group together certain ideas. If we discover a new idea which is, by these same principles, linked to the preceding ones, we are determined to understand it within the group, as though it had been a part of it all along.[15] Lastly, in the case of natural relations, each one of the three principles designates some ideas and produces an easy transition from one to another.

It is true that it is often more difficult to understand the action of the principles. First of all, the principles have other effects, which we have not yet studied, doubling up the preceding ones. These are abstract ideas, philosophical modes and relations. Of course, in the case of abstract ideas the difficulty is not great, because the only difference between abstract and general ideas is that in the case of the former two resemblances intervene and are distinctly apprehended.[16] The problem is rather with philosophical modes and relations. And philosophical relations are to natural relations what modes are to substances. Everything happens, then, as though the principles of association were abandoning their primary, *selective* role, and as though something other than these principles assumed this role and was designating and choosing the appropriate impressions of sensation. This something other is affectivity and circumstance. Thus, philosophical relations are different from natural relations, precisely because they are formed outside the limits of natural selection. As for the impression of reflection, it comes from ideas that are arbitrarily connected within the imagination; we do not find it appropriate to compare these ideas, but only in virtue of a particular circumstance.[17] Similarly, in the case of modes, the impressions of sensations, that is, the ideas from which the impression of reflection proceeds, are no longer tied together by means of contiguity and causality; they are "dispers'd in different subjects." Or, at least, contiguity and causality are no longer considered as "the foundation of the complex idea." "The idea of a dance is an instance of the first kind of modes; that of beauty of the second."[18] In brief, we can see that the principle of association reduces itself to its second, *constitutive* role, while circumstance or affectivity holds now the first role.

Finally, we must make a special place for causality. Hume thinks that belief depends on the two principles of experience and habit.[19] But what are these two doing on the list? To understand this, we must remember that the effect of the principle of causality is not only a relation but is rather an inference according to that relation. Causality is the only relation for which there is inference. Paradoxically, what we must call here natural relation is the inference *according* to the relation. This is why Hume says that, in studying inference before explaining the relation, we are in appearance only reversing the normal order.[20] But if it is true that the nature of relations, as natural relations, depends on the nature of inference, it is still the case that the inference is according to relations; in other words, natural relations in one sense presuppose philosophical relations: it is *as a consequence* of their constant conjunction within experience that objects are necessarily connected in the imagination.[21] The particular situation of causality suffices to convince us that, under this category, natural and philosophical relations are not so easily distributed as they were in the previous case. In effect, everything now happens as though each of the two roles of the principle was embodied in a different principle. The principle of experience is selective: it presents or designates a "repetition of like objects in like relations of succession and contiguity. . . ."[22]

This is what causality is as a philosophical relation: the effect of experience is not even an impression of reflection, since the principle is purely selective. On the contrary, the principle of habit is constitutive, but only at a later stage: being an effect, it has a natural relation or an impression of reflection which is anticipation and belief. As we go from relation to inference, from philosophical relations to natural relations, we switch levels. We must, in a certain sense, start from zero, if only to recover on this other level all the results, albeit enriched, that we have already obtained.[23] Causality will always be defined in two combined ways, "either as a *philosophic* or as a *natural* relation; either as a comparison of two ideas, or as an association betwixt them."[24]

Now the entire difficulty is this: since the two aspects of the principle are embodied in two distinct principles, the second aspect always follows the first, without however depending on it. As a matter of fact, habit can create for itself an equivalent experience; it can invoke fictional repetitions that render it independent of reality.

Be that as it may, the role of the principles of association is to constitute an impression of reflection, on the basis of designated impressions of sensation. *The role of the principles of passion is the same.* The difference between them is that in the second case the chosen impressions are pleasures and pains; but from the point of view of pleasures and pains, the principle still acts as a "natural impulse" or as an "instinct" producing an impression of reflection. However, a new exception must not go unnoticed: there are passions born of their principles, without these principles causing them to go through preliminary pleasures and pains. Such is the case of properly physiological needs, as for example, hunger, thirst, and sexual desire: "These passions, properly speaking, produce good and evil, and proceed not from them, like the other affections."[25]

Having said this, Hume goes on to distinguish two kinds of passions: "By direct passions I understand such as arise immediately from good or evil, from pain or pleasure. By indirect such as proceed from the same principles, but by the conjunction of other qualities."[26] In this sense, any passion always has a cause, in an idea that excites it, an impression from which it proceeds, or in pleasures or pains that are *distinct* from the passion itself. Of whatever kind, the passions always exist in an impression of reflection or in a particular emotion; whether agreeable or disagreeable, the emotion stems from a distinct pain or a distinct pleasure. But, from here on, we are faced with two cases, two kinds of impressions of reflection or two kinds of emotion: those who turn the mind toward good or evil and toward the pleasure or the pain from which they proceed; and those others who turn the mind toward the idea of an object they themselves produce.[27] These are two different kinds of principles and two different kinds of impressions of reflection. Sometimes the principle of the passions is a "primitive instinct" by means of which a mind that has experienced emotion tends to obtain the good and to avoid evil;[28] or at other times, the principle is a natural organization assigning to an emotion a certain idea, "which (the emotion) never fails to produce."[29] That is how direct and indirect passions are distinguished from each other. There are as many direct passions as there are modes of good and evil giving rise to passions: when good and evil are certain, we have joy or sadness; when they are uncertain, we have hope or fear; when they are merely entertained, we have desire and aversion; when they depend on us, we have the will.[30] We distinguish as many indirect passions as there are emotions producing the idea of an object. But among them, two pairs are indeed fundamental: pride and humility, occurring when agreeable or disagreeable emotions produce an idea of the self; love and hate, occurring when the same emotions produce the idea of another person.

Why are the last mentioned passions called "indirect"? It is because, insofar as the impression of reflection produces an idea, the impression of sensation giving rise to it must be born of an object linked to this idea. For there to be pride, the pleasure giving rise to the passion must find its source in an object connected with us.

> 'tis the beauty or deformity of our person, houses, equipage,
> or furniture, by which we are render'd either vain or humble.
> The same qualities, when transfer'd to subjects, which bear
> us no relation, influence not in the smallest degree either of
> these affections.[31]

In this sense, indirect passions proceed from good and evil, "but in conjunction with other qualities": a relation of an idea must be added to the relation of impressions. In pride, "[t]he quality, which operates on the passion, produces separately an impression of resembling it; the subject, to which the quality adheres, is related to self, the object of the passion."[32] The principles of indirect passions can produce their effect only when assisted by the principles of association, at least by contiguity and causality.[33] No doubt, direct and indirect passions do not exclude one another; on the contrary, their respective principles are combined:

> But supposing that there is an immediate impression of pain or pleasure, and *that* arising from an object related to ourselves or others, this does not prevent the propensity or aversion, with the consequent emotions, but by concurring with certain dormant principles of the human mind, excites the new impressions of pride and humility, love or hatred. That propensity, which unites us to the object, or separates us from it, still continues to operate, but in conjunction with the *indirect* passions, which arise from a double relation of impressions and ideas.[34]

The immediate originality of Hume's theory is in the presentation of the differences between direct and indirect passions as a duality, and in the making of this duality into a method for the study of passions in general, instead of understanding or engendering the ones on the basis of the others. Hume's theory of the passions is original because it does not present the passions as a primary movement or as a primary force to be followed by the philosopher, *more geometrico*, in its increasing complexity as other factors intervene (the representation of the object, the imagination, the competition between men, etc.). Hume presented the passions as a process that in itself is simple, although the philosopher, like a physicist, considers it composite and made up of two distinct parts. We are not faced with a logical or mathematical deduction of the passions, but rather with a physical decomposition of them and of the passional movement. But is it not the case that the understanding and the passions are themselves the products of a decomposition and of the division of an already simple movement?

> Human nature being compos'd of two principal parts, which are requisite in all its actions, the affections and understand-

ing; 'tis certain, that the blind motions of the former, without the direction of the latter, incapacitate men for society: And it may be allow'd us to consider separately the effects, that result from the separate operations of these two component parts of the mind. The same liberty may be permitted to moral, which is allow'd to natural philosophers; and 'tis very usual with the latter to consider any motion as compounded and consisting of two parts separate from each other, tho' at the same time they acknowledge it to be in itself uncompounded and inseparable.[35]

Hume's entire philosophy (in fact, empiricism in general) is a kind of "physicalism." As a matter of fact, one must find a *fully* physical usage for principles whose nature is *only* physical. As Kant observes, principles in Hume's text have an exclusively physical and empirical nature. We did not mean anything else when we defined the empirical problem in opposition to a transcendental deduction and also to a psychological genesis. The question of empiricism, "how does the subject constitute itself within the given?", suggests that we distinguish two things: on one hand, that the necessary recourse to principles for the understanding of subjectivity is affirmed; but on the other, that the agreement between principles and the given within which the principles constitute the subject is given up. The principles of experience are not principles for the objects of experience, they do not guarantee the reproduction of objects within experience. Obviously, such a situation is possible for principles only if one finds an equally physical usage for them—one that would be necessary in virtue of the question raised. Now, this physical usage is well determined. Human nature is the transformed mind. But this transformation will be apprehended as indivisible in relation to the mind that undergoes it, because in this case the mind functions as a whole. On the contrary, the same transformation will be apprehended as subject to fragmentation in relation to the principles that produce it as their effect. Finally, we can present the complement of this idea: the subject is indeed the activated mind; but this activation will be apprehended as the mind's passivity in relation to the principles producing it, and as an activity in relation to the mind that undergoes it.

Thus, the subject is decomposed into as many imprints as there are imprints left in the mind by the principles. The subject is decomposed into impressions of reflection, that is, into the impressions left by the principles. It is still the case, however, that, in relation to the mind whose transformation is brought about by the joint operation of the principles, the subject itself is indivisible, nonfragmentable, active, and global. Therefore, in order to reconcile the two points of view, it is not enough to say that the principles have parallel actions; it is not enough to show that they have a common characteristic, that is, the constitution of an impression of reflection based on impressions of sensation. Nor is it enough to show that they implicate one another and that they mutually presuppose one another under different aspects. Each one must be finally and absolutely subordinated to the others. The elements resulting from the decomposition cannot have the same value: there is always a right side and a left side. On this point, we know Hume's reply: the relations find their direction and their sense in the passion; association presupposes projects, goals, intentions, occasions, an entire practical life and affectivity. *Given particular circumstances and the needs of the moment, the passions are capable of replacing the principles of association in their primary role, and of assuming their selective role. They are capable because the principles do not select impressions of sensation without having already been submitted by themselves to the necessities of practical life, and to the most general and most constant needs.* In brief, the principles of the passions are absolutely primary. Between association and the passions we find the same relation that we also find between the possible and the real, once we admit that the real precedes the possible. Association gives the subject a possible structure, but only the passions can give it being and existence. In its relation to the passions, the association finds its sense and its destiny. We should not forget that, in Hume, literally, belief is *for the sake* of sympathy, and causality, *for the sake* of property. Hume often talks about a critique of relations; he presents in fact a theory of the understanding as a critique of relations. Actually, *it is not the relation which is subject to the critique, but rather representation. Hume shows that representation cannot be a criterion for the relations. Relations are not the object of a representation, but the means of an activity.* The same critique, which takes the relation away from representation, gives it back to practice. What is denounced and criticized is the idea that the subject can be a knowing subject. Associationism exists for the sake of utilitarianism. Association does not define a knowing subject; on the contrary, it defines a set of possible means for a practical subject for which all real ends belong to the moral, passional, political, and economic order. Thus, this subordination of association to the passions already manifests within human nature a kind of secondary purposiveness, which prepares us for the problem of the primary purposiveness, that is, for the problem of the agreement between human nature and nature.

CONCLUSION

·

PURPOSIVENESS

PRINCIPLES ACCORDING TO their nature fix the mind in two very different ways. The principles of association establish natural relations among ideas forming inside the mind an entire network similar to a system of channels. No longer do we move accidentally from one idea to another. One idea naturally introduces another on the basis of a principle; ideas naturally follow one another. In short, under the influence of association, imagination becomes reason and the fancy finds constancy. We have seen all of this. Hume, however, makes an important remark: were the mind fixed in this way only, there will never be, nor could there ever have been, morality. This is the first argument which shows that morality does not stem from reason. One must not confuse, in effect, relation and direction. Relations establish a movement between ideas, but this is a to-and-fro movement, such that an idea leads to another only insofar as the latter rightfully leads back to the first: the movement occurs in both directions. Being external to their terms, how would relations be able to determine the priority of one term over the other, or the subordination of one to the other? But it is obvious that action does not tolerate such an equivocation: it needs a starting point, an origin, something which would also be its end, or something beyond which we need not go. Relations, by themselves, would suffice to make the action eternally possible, but they cannot account for the actual per-

·

formance of the action. There is action only through sense or direction (*sens*), and morality is like action. In its resemblance to action, morality circumvents relations. Is it morally the same to be mean to someone who was good to me and nice to someone who wronged me?[1] To recognize that it is not the same thing, despite the fact that the relation of contrariety is the same, is to recognize a radical difference between morality and reason. One could, of course, say that among relations causality already contains within its own synthesis of time a principle of irreversibility. Undoubtedly this is true, and causality is indeed privileged among all relations; but the real question is to know which effect *interests me* and makes me seek out its cause. "It can never in the least concern us to know, that such objects are causes, and such others effects, if both the causes and effects be indifferent to us."[2]

The mind, therefore, must be determined in some other way. The principles of the passions should designate certain impressions, rendering them the ends of our activity. Literally, it is no longer a matter of placing bounds around the mind or of tying it up, but rather of nailing it down. It is no longer a matter of fixed relations, but of centers of fixation. Within the mind, there are impressions which we call pleasures and pains. But that pleasure is good and pain bad, that we tend toward pleasure and push away pain—these facts do not inhere in pain and pleasure themselves; this is why the principles belong here. This is the primary fact beyond which we need not go: "If you push your inquiries further and desire a reason *why he hates pain*, it is impossible he can ever give any. This is an ultimate end, and is never referred to any other object."[3]

By making pleasure into an end, the principles of the passions give action its principle, making thereby the prospect of pleasure a motive for the action.[4] We find thus the link between action and relation. The essence of action is found in the nexus between means and end. To act is to assemble means in order to realize an end. But this nexus is very different from a relation. Undoubtedly, it includes the causal relation, since all means are causes, and all ends, effects. Causality, enjoys a considerable privilege over other relations.

A merchant is desirous of knowing the sum total of his accounts with any person: Why? but that he may learn what sum will have the same *effects* in paying his debt, and going to market, as all the particular articles taken together. Abstract or demonstrative reasoning, therefore, never influences any of our actions, but only as it directs our judgment concerning causes and effects.[5]

But for a cause to be considered as a means, the effect which it brings about must interest us, that is, the idea of the effect must first of all be posited as an end for our action. The means exceeds the cause: the effect must be thought of as a good, the subject who projects it must have a tendency to achieve it. The relation of means to end is not merely causal; it is rather a kind of utility. The useful is defined by its appropriation or by its disposition "to promote a good." A cause is a means only for a subject that tends to achieve the effect of this cause.

Now, what are these subjective tendencies of achieving and promoting goods? They are the effects of the principles of affectivity, impressions of reflection and of the passions. Similarly, the useful is not only a cause considered in its relation to an effect that we posit as something good. It is also a tendency to promote that good or a quality considered in relation to the circumstances that agree with it. For there are two ways to understand human qualities, such as anger, prudence, audacity, discretion, etc.: generically, as possible universal responses to given circumstances; and differentially, as given character traits which may or may not agree with possible circumstances.[6] It is from the latter point of view that character traits are useful or harmful.

> The best character, indeed, were it not rather too perfect for human nature, is that which is not swayed by temper of any kind, but alternately employs enterprise and caution, as each is *useful* to the particular purpose intended. . . . Fabius, says Machiavelli, was cautious; Scipio enterprising; and both succeeded because the situation of the Roman affairs, during the command of each, was peculiarly adapted to his genius, but both would have failed had these situations been reversed. He is happy whose circumstances suit his temper; but he is more excellent who can suit his temper to any circumstances.[7]

The utility, which designates the relation between means and end, also designates the relation between individuality and the historical situation. Utilitarianism is as much an evaluation of historical acts as it is a theory of instrumental action. We do not call things only "useful," but also passions, feelings, and characters. Indeed, our moral judgment is not brought to bear on the utility of things, but, in a way that must be specified, on the utility of characters.[8] And this is the second argument for the fact that morality as a guide to action is not attached to reason. Reason has indeed a double role. It helps us to know causes and effects, and it tells us also whether or not "we chuse means insufficient for the design'd end"; but even so, an end has to be projected.[9] Again, it is reason that permits us to know and to untangle the circumstances; but the feeling produced in virtue of the totality of circumstances depends on a "natural constitution of the mind." "[I]t is requisite a *sentiment* should here display itself in order to give a preference to the useful above the pernicious tendencies."[10]

It is not by accident that morality has a right to speak on precisely those subjects with respect to which reason remains silent. How does it speak? What kind of discourse does it maintain about ends and characters? We do not know yet, but at least we do know this:

> Reason, being cool and disengaged, is no motive to action,
> and directs only the impulse received from appetite or in-
> clination by showing us the means of attaining happiness
> and avoiding misery. Taste, as it gives pleasure or pain, and
> thereby constitutes happiness or misery, becomes a motive
> to action and is the first spring or impulse to desire and
> volition.[11]

Our first conclusion must then be that the combined principles make the mind itself into a subject and the fancy into a human nature. They establish a subject within the given, because a mind equipped with ends and relations—with relations responding to those ends—is a subject. There is, however, still a difficulty: the subject is constituted with the help of principles inside the given, but it is constituted as an entity that goes beyond that given. The subject is the effect of principles in the mind, but it is the mind that becomes subject; it is the mind that, in the last analysis, transcends itself. In short, we must realize both that the subject is *constituted by means of principles* and that it is *grounded in the fancy*. Hume says so himself in relation to knowledge: memory, the senses, and understanding are all grounded in the imagination.

But what does the mind do after becoming subject? It *"advises certain ideas rather than others."* "To transcend" means exactly this. The mind is animated when the principles fix it, as they establish relations between ideas; it is animated when they activate it, in the sense that they give to the vividness of impressions certain laws of communication, distribution, and allotment. In fact, *a relation between two ideas is also the quality by means of which an impression communicates to that idea something of its vividness.*[12] The fact is that vividness is not *in itself* a product of principles; being a characteristic of impressions, it is the property and the fact of fancy—its irreducible and immediate datum, to the extent that it is the origin of the mind.

Within the domain of knowledge, then, we seek a formula for the activity of the mind having become subject, that is, a formula that would agree with all the effects of association. For Hume, the formula is this: to transcend is always to move from the known to the unknown.[13] We call this operation the schematism of the mind (general rules) and we know that it is the essence of this schematism to be extensive. All knowledge is indeed a system of relations between parts, such that we can determine one part by reference to another. One of Hume's most important ideas—one that he will use particularly against the possibility of any cosmology or theology—is that there is no intensive knowledge; all possible knowledge is extensive and between parts. This extensive schematism, however, has two characteristics which correspond to the two kinds of relations: matters of fact and relations among ideas. Hume suggests that, in knowledge, either we move from known to unknown circumstances, or we proceed from known to unknown relations. Here we find a distinction, dear to Hume, between proof and certainty. The first operation, that of proof or probability, develops under the action of principles a schematism of the *cause* (which we have sufficiently examined in the preceding chapters); but how is the schematism of the second operation formed? The first is essentially physical, the second, essentially mathematical. "A speculative reasoner concerning triangles or circles considers the several known and given relations of the parts of these figures, and thence infers some unknown relation which is dependent on the former."[14]

This second schematism seems to relate not to causes but to general ideas. The function of general ideas is not so much to be ideas but rather to be the rule for the production of the ideas that we need.[15] In the case of causality, we produce an object as an object of belief by means of another particular object and in conformity with the rules of observation. The mathematical function of general ideas is different: it consists in producing an idea as an object of certainty, by means of another idea which is apprehended as a rule of construction.

> [W]hen we mention any great number, such as a thousand, the mind has generally no adequate idea of it, but only a power of producing such an idea, by its adequate idea of the decimals, under which the number is comprehended.[16]

However, this schematism of knowledge in general, under these two aspects, is extensive not only in the sense that it goes from one part to another but is also extensive in the sense that it is *excessive*. Vividness, in fact, is not the product of principles; impressions of sensations are the product of principles; impressions of sensations are the origin of the mind and the property of the fancy. As soon as relations are established, these impressions tend to communicate their vividness to all ideas tied to them.[17] In Hume's empiricism, this resembles somehow the possibles, which in the case of rationalism tend with all their might toward Being. The fact is, though, that not all relations are equivalent: from the point of view of human nature, we know that not all relations have the same effect "in reinforcing and making our ideas vivid," and that any legitimate belief must necessarily pass through causality. Undoubtedly, any relation between two ideas is also the quality by means of which the impression enlivens the idea to which it is linked; but it is also necessary that the idea be linked in a firm, constant, and invariable way.[18] Moreover, impressions do not merely necessitate relations; they also feign and fabricate relations in the course of encounters. The subject, then, is here subject to pressures, being tormented by mirages and solicited by fancy. Its passions and dispositions of the moment lead it to second these fictions. In a word, we are not only a subject, we are something else as well; we are also a self, which is always a slave to its origin. The fact is that there exist illegitimate beliefs and absurd general ideas. The principles establish relations between ideas, and these relations are also, in the case of impressions, the rules for the communication of their vividness. It is still necessary, however, that vividness conforms without exception to these rules. This is why, within the schematism of knowledge, there are always excessive rules waiting to be corrected by other rules: the schematism of the cause must conform to experience, and the schematism of general ideas must conform to space, both in geometrical structure and arithmetical unit—in other words, in the two aspects that define space.[19] An entire polemic between the subject and the fancy is thus carried out inside the self, or rather inside the subject itself. An entire polemic is carried out *between the principles of human nature and the vividness of the imagination*, or between principles and fictions. We know how, for every object of knowledge, the fiction can effectively be corrected, even if it were to be reborn with the next object. But we also know how, in the case of the world in general within which all objects become known, fiction takes over the principles and bends them radically to its own service.

Let us examine now the activity of the mind in the case of the passions. The principles of the passions fix the mind by giving it ends; they also activate it because the prospects of these ends are at the same time motives and dispositions to act, inclinations, and particular interests. In short, they bring about a "natural constitution" to our mind and an entire play of the passions. Within the mind, the principles constitute affections, giving them "*a proper limited object*."[20] However, this object is always caught within a system of circumstances and relations. It is precisely here that we find the fundamental difference between knowledge and the passions: in the case of the passions, at least by right, all relations and all circumstances are already given. Agrippina is Nero's mother.

> But when Nero killed Agrippina, all the relations between himself and the person, and all the circumstances of the fact, were previously known to him; but the motive of revenge or fear or interest prevailed in his savage heart. . . .[21]

Thus, the natural constitution of the mind under the influence of the principles of the passions does not only involve the movement of an affection seeking out its object, it also involves the reaction of a mind responding to the supposedly known totality of circumstances and relations. In other words, our inclinations form *general views* upon their objects. They are not led by particular connections only, or by the attraction of a pleasure which happens to be present.[22] We find thus in the case of the passions, as much as in the case of knowledge albeit in a different way, an ineluctable datum of the fancy. The affection, which seeks out its object, forms general views upon this very object, because both are reflected in the imagination and the fancy. The principles of the passions fix the mind only if, within the mind, the passions resonate, extend themselves, and succeed in being reflected. The reaction of the mind to the set of circumstances and the reflection of the passions in the mind are one and the same; the reaction is productive, and the reflection is called "invention."

> It is wisely ordained by nature that private connections should commonly prevail over universal views and considerations, otherwise our affections and actions would be dissipated and lost for want of a proper limited object . . . but still we know here, as in all the senses, to correct these inequalities by reflection, and retain a general standard of vice and virtue, founded chiefly on general usefulness.[23]

General interest is thus invented: it is the resonance within the imagination of the particular interest and the movement of a passion that transcends its own partiality. General interest exists only by means of the imagination, artifice, or the fancy; nonetheless, it enters the natural constitution of the mind as a feeling for humanity or as culture. It is in fact the reaction of the mind to the totality of circumstances and relations. It provides action with a rule and it is in the name of this rule that it can be pronounced good or bad *in general*. We may consequently condemn Nero. Thus, the activity of the mind is grounded, in the case of the passions as well as in the case of knowledge, in the fancy. A moral schematism therefore exists. But the difference between schematisms does not disappear: the moral schematism is no longer an extensive schematism; it is an intensive one. The activity of the mind no longer consists in going from one part to another, from known to unknown relations, or from known to unknown circumstances. The activity of the mind consists now in reacting to the supposed totality of known circumstances and relations.

> From circumstances and relations, known or supposed, the former leads us to the discovery of the concealed and unknown. After all circumstances and relations are laid before us, the latter makes us feel from the whole a new sentiment of blame or approbation.[24]

The circle as an object of knowledge is a relation of parts; it is the locus of points situated at an equal distance from a common point called a "center." For example, as an object of aesthetic feeling, this figure is taken as a whole to which the mind reacts according to its natural constitution.[25] We recall Hume's text on knowledge, according to which the rules of the understanding are in the last analysis grounded in the imagination. To this text, another text now corresponds, according to which the rules of the passions are also, albeit in the last analysis, grounded in the imagination.[26] In both cases, the fancy finds itself at the foundation of a world, that is, of the world of culture and the world of distinct and continuous existence. We know that, in the schematisms of morality and knowledge, we find both excessive and corrective rules. But these two kinds of rules do not have with respect to each other the same kind of relation in knowledge and in morality. The excessive rules of knowledge openly contradict the principles of association; to correct them amounts to denouncing their fiction. A distinct and continuous world is, from the point of view of the principles, the general residue of this fiction, being situated at a level that makes it impossible to be corrected. As for the excessive moral rules, they undoubtedly constrain the passions; they also sketch out a wholly fictitious world. But this world conforms to the principles of the passions, frustrating only the limiting character of their effect. Fiction integrates into a whole all those passions that excluded each other because they represented particular interests. It establishes therefore (along with the general interest) an adequation of the passions to their principles, of effects taken together to their cause, and of an equality between the effect of the principles and the principles themselves. Consequently, a harmony is established between fiction and the principles of the passions. This is why the problem of the relation between the principles of human nature in general and the fancy can be understood and resolved only from the particular perspective of the relation between principles themselves. In the case of knowledge, we must believe in accordance with causality, but also believe in distinct and continuous existence; human nature does not allow us to choose between the two, despite the fact that the two are contradictory from the point of view of the principles of association. This is because these principles themselves do not contain the secret of human nature. And this is to say, once again, that the association is *for the sake of* the passions. The principles of human nature act separately within the mind; nevertheless they constitute a subject that functions as a whole. Abstract ideas are subjected to the needs of the subject, whereas relations are subjected to its ends. We call "*intentional purposiveness*" the unity of a subject that functions as a whole. To try to understand associationism as a psychology of knowledge is to lose its meaning. The fact is that associationism is the theory of all that is practice, action, morality, and law.

We have tried to show how the two aspects of the subject are actually one and the same: the subject is the product of principles within the mind, but it is also the mind that transcends itself. The mind becomes subject by means of its principles, so that the subject is at once constituted by the principles and grounded in the fancy. How so? In itself, the mind is not subject: it is a given collection of impressions and separate ideas. Impressions are defined by their vividness, and ideas, as reproductions of impressions. This means that, in itself, the mind has two fundamental characteristics: *resonance* and *vividness*. Recall the metaphor that likens the mind to a percussion instrument. When does it become subject? It becomes subject when *its vividness is mobilized in such a way that the part characterized by vividness (impression) communicates it to another part (idea)*, and also, *when all the parts taken together resonate in the act of producing something new*. Belief and invention are the two modes of transcendence and we can see their relation to the original characteristics of the mind. These two modes present themselves as the modifications of the mind caused by the principles, or as the effects of the principles within the mind: principles of association and principles of passion.

We should not ask what principles, are, but rather what they do.

They are not entities; they are functions. They are defined by their effects. These effects amount to this: the principles constitute, within the given, a subject that invents and believes. In this sense, the principles are principles of human nature. To believe is to anticipate. To communicate to an idea the vividness of the impression to which it is attached is to anticipate; it is to transcend memory and the senses. For this purpose, there must already be relations between ideas: it must be the case, for example, that heat and fire are conjoined. And this does not imply only the given but also the action of principles, experience as a principle, resemblance, and contiguity. And that is not all; it must be the case that in seeing fire at a distance we believe that there is heat—and this implies habit. The fact is that the given will never justify relations between its separate parts—not even in similar cases—nor would it justify the transition from one part to another.

> May I not clearly and distinctly conceive that a body, falling from the clouds, and which, in all other respects, resembles snow, has yet the taste of salt or feeling of fire? Is there any more intelligible proposition than to affirm, that all the trees will flourish in December . . . ?[27]

Not only does the subject anticipate, but it conserves itself,[28] that is, it reacts, whether by instinct or by invention, to every part of the given. Here again, the fact is that the given never joins together its separate elements into a whole. In short, as we believe and invent, we turn the given itself into a *nature*. At this point Hume's philosophy reaches its ultimate point: Nature conforms to being. Human nature conforms to nature—but in what sense? Inside the given, we establish relations and we form totalities. But *the latter* do not depend on the given, but rather on the principles we know; they are purely functional. And the functions agree with the hidden powers on which the given depends, although we do not know these powers. We call "purposiveness" this agreement between intentional finality and nature. This agreement can only be thought; and it is undoubtedly the weakest and emptiest of thoughts. Philosophy must constitute itself as the theory of what we are doing, not as a theory of what there is. What we do has its principles; and being can only be grasped as the object of a synthetic relation with the very principles of what we do.

NOTES

Translator's Introduction: Deleuze, Empiricism, and the Struggle for Subjectivity

1. See G. Deleuze, *Le Bergsonisme* (Paris: Presses Universitaires de France, 1966); Hugh Tomlinson and Barbara Habberjam, trs., *Bergsonism* (New York: Zone Books, 1988).

2. See G. Deleuze, Martin Joughin, tr., *Expressionism in Philosophy: Spinoza* (New York: Zone Books, 1990); see also G. Deleuze, *Le Pli: Leibniz et le Baroque* (Paris: Minuit, 1988).

3. J.-J. Lecercle, *Philosophy Through the Looking-Glass: Language, Nonsense, Desire* (London: Hutchinson, 1985).

4. For an updated, yet not exhaustive, list of Deleuze's publications, see Ronald Bogue, *Deleuze and Guattari* (New York: Routledge, 1989), 180–185, 186–187. See *Magazine Littéraire*, September 1988, no. 257, 64–65; and *Substance*, 44/45 (1984).

5. See *Histoire de la philosophie* (Paris: Hachette, 1972–73), 4:65–78. This collective work has been reedited in *Marabout Université*, under the title *La Philosophie*, F. Châtelet et al., eds. (Verviers: Marabout, 1979), vol. 2:226–239.

6. See, for example, "Lettre à Michel Cressole," in M. Cressole, *Deleuze* (Paris: Editions Universitaires, 1973), p. 110, and G. Deleuze, Claire Parnet, *Dialogues*, Hugh Tomlinson and Barbara Habberjam, trs. (New York: Columbia University Press, 1987), pp. 14–15; 54–59. See also "Signes et événements," interview with R. Bellour and F. Ewald, *Magazine Littéraire*, September 1988, no. 257, p. 16.

7. See G. Deleuze and F. Guattari, *A Thousand Plateaus: Capitalism and Schizophrenia*, B. Massumi, tr. (Minneapolis: University of Minnesota Press, 1987), pp. 233–309.

8. See *infra*, 98–101.

9. On "minoritarian discourse," see especially *A Thousand Plateaus: Capitalism and Schizophrenia*, pp. 100–110; see also G. Deleuze and F. Guattari, *Kafka: Toward a Minor Literature*, Dana Polan, tr. (Minneapolis: University of Minnesota Press, 1986), pp. 16–27.

10. On series and serialization, see G. Deleuze, *The Logic of Sense*, Mark Lester with Charles Stivale, trs., Constantin V. Boundas, ed. (New York: Columbia University Press, 1990), pp. 36–47.

11. For Deleuze's critique of transcendental philosophy, see, for example, *The Logic of Sense*, pp. 109–117 see also *infra*.

12. *Dialogues*, p. vii.

13. V. Descombes, *Modern French Philosophy*, L. Scott-Fox and J.M. Harding, trs. (Cambridge: Cambridge University Press, 1980), pp. 152; 155.

14. J. Derrida, *Writing and Difference*, Alan Bass, tr. and introd. (Chicago: University of Chicago Press, 1978), p. 151.

15. *Modern French Philosophy*, p. 161.

16. See V. Descombes, *Modern French Philosophy*, pp. 152 ff.

17. G. Deleuze, "Lettre à Cressole," p. 110.

18. See, for example, *Dialogues*, p. 12.

19. See *The Logic of Sense*, pp. 101–102.

20. See *The Logic of Sense*, pp. 109–117 and also 301–320.

21. See G. Deleuze, *Foucault*, Sean Hand, tr. (Minneapolis: University of Minnesota Press, 1988), pp. 107–113; and G. Deleuze, *Le Pli: Leibniz et le Baroque*, pp. 20–37.

22. I have learned a great deal from, and admired a great deal, John Caputo's *Radical Hermeneutics: Repetition, Deconstruction and the Hermeneutic Project* (Bloomington: Indiana University Press, 1987); but, in the last analysis, it seems to me that his version of radical hermeneutics should not be stored up in old hermeneutic bottles; I am afraid, though, that in his cellar Caputo has kept a lot of these bottles.

23. See *Foucault*, p. 114. On intensive forces, see G. Deleuze, *Différence et répétition* (Paris: Presses Universitaires de France, 1985), pp. 286–336.

24. See *Bergsonism*, pp. 91–113; see also G. Deleuze, *Cinema 1: The Movement-Image*, Hugh Tomlinson and Barbara Habberjam, trs. (Minneapolis: University of Minnesota Press, 1986), pp. 56–70.

25. See *Foucault*, pp. 94–123; see also *Le Pli: Leibniz et le Baroque*, pp. 27–37.

26. See, for example, *Différence et répétition* (Paris: Presses Universitaires de France, 1968), pp. 213 ff.

27. See *infra*, pp. 107–109.

28. *Infra*, pp. 112 ff.

29. *Infra*, p. 105.

30. *Infra*, pp. 87–88.

31. See *An Enquiry*, p. 21, note. Deleuze's acceptance of the equivalence of the terms "innate" and "primitive" testifies to his subscription to a strong phenomenalist reading of Hume.

32. For Deleuze's theory of repetition, and for the relation between repetition and difference, see *Différence et répétition, passim*.

33. *Infra*, pp. 120–121.

34. *Infra*, pp. 41–42. A general rule or norm is a system of goal-oriented means. It is an "extensive" rule whenever it helps transcend the limited number of cases which give rise to it; it is a "corrective" rule whenever it corrects our feelings and lifts our attention from our particular circumstances.

35. The idea in search of a concept has been discussed in *Différence et répétition*, chap. 4, but also in *The Critical Philosophy of Kant*, Hugh Tomlinson and Barbara Habberjam, trs. (Minneapolis: University of Minnesota Press, 1984), p. 56.

36. For the often overlooked difference between "indeterminacy" and "undecidability," see J. Derrida, *Limited Inc* (Evanston: Northwestern University Press, 1988), pp. 115 ff.

37. Calvin O. Schrag, for instance, has argued for the reprieve of the praxiological subject, and John Fekete complained about the eclipse of the critical memory of a subject which is "never yet p." See C. O. Schrag, *Communicative Praxis and the Space of Subjectivity* (Bloomington: Indiana University Press, 1986), esp. Part 2; see also J. Fekete, *The Structural Allegory: Reconstructive Encounters with the New French Thought* (Minneapolis: University of Minnesota Press, 1984), p. xviii.

38. "Neo-Structuralism" is the label coined by Manfred Frank and made to designate the theory of those that we used to call "poststructuralists" or "New French Theorists". See his *What is Neo-Structuralism?* Sabine Wilke and Richard Gray, trs. (Minneapolis: University of Minnesota Press, 1989).

39. In this respect, Deleuze's approach to the question of the Self and the Other is more nuanced. In fact, for him, the structure-Other and the structure-Self are contemporaneous. Only the reduction of the Other will permit the disclosure of pre-individual singularities and events behind the structure-Self. The real transcendental field, for Deleuze, requires the epoch of an *altrucide* and a *suicide*. See *The Logic of Sense*, pp. 301–321.

40. Gilles Deleuze, *Foucault*, p. 96.

41. *Foucault*, p. 97.

42. See Manfred Frank, *Die Unhintergehbarkeit von Individualität* (Frankfurt am Main: Suhrkamp, 1986), *passim*.

43. *Infra*, p. 85, p. 86.

44. See *Dialogues*, p. 93.

45. See *Foucault*, p. 106.

46. This is the title of Philippe Hodard's book, published in Paris by Aubier-Montaigne in 1981.

47. Deleuze's most concise discussion of time can be found in *Différence et répétition*, pp. 96–128.

48. On "repetition," see *Différence et répétition*, pp. 365–390; on "absolute memory," *Foucault*, p. 107; on "assembling" and "subjectivity," see *One Thousand Plateaus*, pp. 264–265; on "becoming-other," see *Dialogues*, pp. 124 ff.

49. *Infra*, pp. 37–40.

50. *Infra*, p. 63.

51. André Cresson and Gilles Deleuze, *Hume, sa vie, son oeuvre avec un exposé de sa philosophie* (Paris: Presses Universitaires de France, 1952), p. 69.

52. *Infra*, p. 100.

53. This decisively Kantian reading of Hume has been critically discussed by Patricia de Martelaere in "Gilles Deleuze, Interprète de Hume," *Revue Philosophique de Louvain* (May 1984), 82:224–248.

54. "Hume," *La Philosophie*, F. Châtelet et al., eds., 2:232.

Chapter One: The Problem of Knowledge and the Problem of Ethics

1. David Hume, *A Treatise of Human Nature*, L. A. Selby-Bigge, ed. (Oxford: Clarendon Press, 1888), p. 405. Hereafter referred to as *Treatise*.

2. *Treatise*, p. 521.

3. *Treatise*, p. 493.

4. *Treatise*, p. 253.

5. *Treatise*, p. 24.

6. *Treatise*, p. 10.

7. *Treatise*, p. 125; Indifference as "primitive situation" of the mind.

8. *Treatise*, p. 10.

9. The *Treatise* contains an essential text: "As all simple ideas may be separated by the imagination, and may be united again in what form it pleases, nothing wou'd be more unaccountable than the operations of that faculty, were it not guided by some universal principles, which render it, in some measure, uniform with itself in all times and places. Were ideas entirely loose and unconnected, chance alone wou'd join them; . . ." p. 10.

10. *Treatise*, pp. 10, 225: ". . . upon [. . .] removal [of the principles] human nature must immediately perish and go to ruin."

11. *Treatise*, pp. 74, 107, 109.

12. *Treatise*, p. 10.

13. *Treatise*, p. 13: ". . . that quality, by which two ideas are connected together in the imagination. . . ."

14. David Hume, *An Enquiry Concerning Human Understanding* (La Salle: Open Court, 1966), p. 58. Hereafter referred to as *An Enquiry*. Purposiveness is the agreement between the principles of human nature and Nature itself. "Here, then, is a kind of pre-established harmony between the cause of nature and the succession of our ideas."

15. David Hume, *Dialogues Concerning Natural Religion*, by Nelson Pike, ed. and commentary (Indianapolis: Bobbs-Merrill, 1970), pp. 97f. Hereafter referred to as *Dialogues*.

16. *Treatise*, p. 13.

17. *Treatise*, pp. 10–11.

18. *Treatise*, p. 13.

19. *Treatise*, p. 260.

20. *Treatise*, p. 35.

21. *Treatise*, p. 146.

22. *Treatise*, p. 237: "In our arrangement of bodies we never fail to place

such as are resembling, in contiguity to each other, or at least in correspondent points of view: Why? but because we feel a satisfaction in joining the relation of contiguity to that of resemblance, or the resemblance of situation to that of qualities." See also *Treatise*, p. 504, note.

23. *Treatise*, p. 165.

24. *Treatise*, p. 164.

25. *Treatise*, p. 406.

26. *Treatise*, p. 405.

27. *Treatise*, p. 167.

28. *Treatise*, pp. 167, 169.

29. *Treatise*, p. 408.

30. *Treatise*, p. 400: "Every object is determin'd by an absolute fate to a certain degree and direction of its motion, and can no more depart from that precise line, in which it moves, than it can convert itself into an angel, or spirit, or any superior substance. *The actions, therefore, of matter are to be regarded as instances of necessary actions*; and whatever is in this respect on the same footing with matter, must be acknowledg'd to be necessary." The italics are mine.

31. *Treatise*, p. 273.

32. Auguste Comte, *The Positive Philosophy*, H. Martineau, tr. (New York: Belford, Clarke, 188-), p. 384.

33. *Treatise*, p. 19: "That is a contradiction in terms; and even implies the flattest of all contradictions, *viz.* that 'tis possible for the same thing both to be and not to be."

34. *Treatise*, p. 168.

35. Jean Laporte has shown adequately the immediately contradictory character that a practice expressed as an idea assumes in Hume's writings. In this sense, the impossible formula of abstraction is: how could we turn 1 into 2? And the impossible formula of the necessary connection is: how could we turn 2 into 1? Se his *Le problème de l'abstraction* (Paris: Presses Universitaires de France, 1940).

36. See *Treatise*, p. 264, on the "forelorn solitude" of the philosopher, and p. 159 on the uselessness of long reasonings.

37. *Treatise*, p. 277.

38. *Treatise*, pp. 628–629.

39. With respect to general ideas, Hume states clearly that to understand his thesis we must first go through the critique. "Perhaps these four reflexions may help to remove all difficulties to the hypothesis I have propos'd concerning abstract ideas, so contrary to that, which has hitherto prevail'd in philosophy. But to tell the truth I place my chief confidence in what I have already prov'd concerning the impossibility of general ideas, according to the common method of explaining them." *Treatise*, p. 24. To understand what an affection of the mind is, we must go through the critique of the psychology of the mind.

40. *Treatise*, p. 165.

41. *Treatise*, p. 162.

42. *Treatise*, p. 179: ". . . reason is nothing but a wonderful and unin-

telligible instinct in our souls, which carries along a certain train of ideas, and endows them with particular qualities. . . ."

43. *Treatise*, p. 187.
44. *Treatise*, p. 583.
45. *Treatise*, p. 8.
46. *Treatise*, p. 37; the italics are mine. See also *Treatise*, p. 287.
47. *Treatise*, p. 636.
48. *Treatise*, pp. 319–320.
49. *Treatise*, p. 317, *An Enquiry*, pp. 89–90.
50. *Treatise*, p. 406: The prisoner "when conducted to the scaffold, foresees his death as certainly from the constancy and fidelity of his guards as from the operation of the ax or wheel." Between moral and physical evidence, there is no difference of nature. See *Treatise*, p. 171.
51. *An Enquiry*, p. 90: "These records of wars, intrigues, factions, and revolutions, are so many collections of experiments, by which the politician or moral philosopher fixes the principles of his science, in the same manner as the physician or natural philosopher becomes acquainted with the nature of plants, minerals, and other external objects, by the experiments which he forms concerning them."
52. *Treatise*, p. 416.
53. *Treatise*, p. 459.
54. *Treatise*, p. 415.
55. *Treatise*, p. 457.
56. *Treatise*, p. 468.
57. *Treatise*, p. 269.
58. *An Enquiry*, p. 173.
59. Conversely, through an appropriate change of state of affairs, understanding investigates itself about the nature of ethics: see *Treatise*, pp. 270–271.
60. *Treatise*, p. 169: "This order wou'd not have been excusable, of first examining our inference from the relation before we had explain'd the relation itself, had it been possible to proceed in a different method."
61. *Treatise*, pp. 468–470.
62. *Treatise*, p. 471; see also David Hume, *An Inquiry Concerning the Principles of Morals*, Charles W. Hendel, ed. and introd. (Indianapolis: Bobbs-Merrill, 1957), p. 150. Hereafter referred to as *Inquiry*.
63. *Treatise*, p. 253: ". . . we must distinguish betwixt personal identity, as it regards our thought or imagination, and as it regards our passion or the concern we take in ourselves."
64. *Treatise*, p. 173.
65. *Treatise*, p. 164.
66. *Treatise*, pp. 135–136.
67. *Treatise*, p. 130.
68. *Dialogues*, pp. 78–79.
69. *Treatise*, p. 175.
70. *Treatise*, p. 484.
71. *Treatise*, p. 497.

72. *Treatise*, p. 579.
73. *Inquiry*, p. 108.

Chapter Two: Cultural World and General Rules

1. David Hume, *A Treatise of Human Nature*, L. A. Selby-Bigge, ed. (Oxford: Clarendon Press, 1888), p. 472: " 'tis only when a character is considered in general, without reference to our particular interest, that it causes such a feeling or sentiment, as denominates it morally good or evil." Hereafter referred to as *Treatise*.
2. *Treatise*, p. 382.
3. *Treatise*, p. 386.
4. *Treatise*, p. 387.
5. *Treatise*, pp. 483–484.
6. *Treatise*, p. 586.
7. *Treatise*, p. 488.
8. *Treatise*, p. 487.
9. *Treatise*, p. 484.
10. *Treatise*, p. 487.
11. *Treatise*, pp. 583, 602–603.
12. *Treatise*, p. 581.
13. *Inquiry*, p. 21.
14. *Treatise*, p. 486.
15. *Treatise*, p. 619: "Those who resolve the sense of morals into original instincts of the human mind, may defend the cause of virtue with sufficient authority; but want the advantage, which those possess, who account for that sense by an extensive sympathy with mankind."
16. *Treatise*, p. 581.
17. *Inquiry*, p. 45.
18. *Treatise*, pp. 483–484.
19. David Hume, "Of Parties in General" in *Political Essays*, Charles W. Hendel, ed. and introd. (Indianapolis: Bobbs-Merrill, 1953), pp. 77–84.
20. *Treatise*, p. 591.
21. *Treatise*, p. 603.
22. *Treatise*, p. 499.
23. *Treatise*, p. 490.
24. *Treatise*, p. 597: "In like manner, therefore, as we establish the *laws of nature*, in order to secure property in society, and prevent the opposition of self-interest; we establish the *rules of good-breeding*, in order to prevent the opposition of men's pride, and render conversation agreeable and inoffensive."
25. *Treatise*, p. 490.
26. *Treatise*, p. 582: "Experience soon teaches us this method of correcting our sentiments, or at least, of correcting our language, where the sentiments are more stubborn and inalterable."
27. *Treatise*, p. 499.
28. *Treatise*, pp. 370–371; see also *Treatise*, p. 370: "the communicated

passion of sympathy sometimes acquires strength from the weakness of its original, and even arises by a transition from affections, which have no existence."

29. *Treatise*, pp. 484–485.

30. *Treatise*, pp. 492–493; pp. 619–620.

31. *Treatise*, p. 492.

32. *Treatise*, p. 489; the italics are mine. In the next chapter, we shall discuss the correct understanding of "in the judgment and understanding."

33. *Treatise*, pp. 619–620: "Those who resolve the sense of morals into original instincts of the human mind, may defend the cause of virtue with sufficient authority; but want the advantage, which those possess, who account for that sense by an extensive sympathy with mankind." "Tho' justice be artificial, the sense of its morality is natural. 'Tis the combination of men, in a system of conduct, which renders any act of justice beneficial to society. But when once it has that tendency, we *naturally* approve of it. . . ."

34. *Treatise*, p. 583.

35. *Treatise*, p. 521: ". . . teach us that we can better satisfy our appetites in an oblique and artificial manner, than by their headlong and impetuous motion."

36. *Treatise*, p. 526: "Whatever restraint they may impose on the passions of men, they are the real offspring of those passions, and are only a more artful and more refin'd way of satisfying them. Nothing is more vigilant and inventive than our passions. . . ."

37. *Treatise*, p. 484: "Tho' the rules of justice be *artificial*, they are not *arbitrary*. Nor is the expression improper to call them *Laws of Nature*."

38. This is the theme of Hume's "A Dialogue"; see *Inquiry*, pp. 141–158.

39. *Treatise*, p. 619.

40. *Treatise*, p. 500.

41. *Inquiry*, section 2.

42. *Treatise*, pp. 516–517.

43. *Treatise*, p. 490.

44. *Treatise*, p. 497.

45. *Inquiry*, pp. 32–33.

46. *Treatise*, pp. 501–502.

47. *Treatise*, pp. 480–481.

48. *Treatise*, p. 504.

49. *Treatise*, p. 508.

50. *Treatise*, pp. 512, 513.

51. *Treatise*, pp. 502, 555.

52. *Treatise*, p. 520. In this sense, the promise names persons. See *Treatise*, p. 555.

53. *Treatise*, p. 535; see also p. 538.

54. *Treatise*, p. 543.

55. *Treatise*, p. 537.

56. *Treatise*, p. 554.

57. *Treatise*, pp. 545–549.

58. *Treatise*, pp. 549–553.
59. *Treatise*, pp. 487–488.
60. *Inquiry*, pp. 25–26; "Of Interest," *Essays, Moral, Political and Literary* (London: Oxford University Press, 1963), p. 305.
61. "Of Interest," *Essays*, p. 309.
62. "Of Interest," *Essays*, p. 307.
63. "Of Commerce," *Essays*, p. 268.
64. Elie Halévy, *The Growth of Philosophic Radicalism*, Mary Morris, tr. (London: Faber and Faber, 1934), Part 1.

Chapter Three: The Power of the Imagination in Ethics and Knowledge

1. *Treatise*, p. 551.
2. *Treatise*, p. 551.
3. *Treatise*, p. 358.
4. *Treatise*, p. 585.
5. *Treatise*, p. 587.
6. *Treatise*, p. 585.
7. *Treatise*, p. 586.
8. *Treatise*, pp. 584–585.
9. David Hume, "Of Tragedy," *Essays, Moral, Political and Literary*, p. 221.
10. "Of Tragedy," *Essays*, pp. 225–226.
11. *Treatise*, p. 408.
12. *Treatise*, p. 12.
13. *Treatise*, pp. 570–571.
14. *Treatise*, p. 572.
15. *Treatise*, pp. 311–312: "It has been observ'd in treating of the understanding, that the distinction, which we sometimes make betwixt a *power* and the *exercise* of it, is entirely frivolous, and that neither man nor any other being ought ever to be thought possest of any ability, unless it be exerted and put in action. But tho' this be strictly true in a just and *philosophical* way of thinking, 'tis certain it is not *the philosophy* of our passions; but that many things operate upon them by means of the idea and supposition of power, independent of its actual exercise."
16. *Treatise*, p. 489; the italics are mine.
17. David Hume, "Of the Standard of Taste," *Hume's Ethical Writings*, Alasdair MacIntyre, ed. and introd. (New York: Collier Books, 1965), pp. 275–295.
18. *Treatise*, pp. 506–507, note 1.
19. *Treatise*, p. 511, note.
20. *Treatise*, p. 506: "We are said to be in possession of any thing, not only when we immediately touch it, but also when we are so situated with respect to it, as to have it in our power to use it; and may move, alter, or destroy it, according to our present pleasure or advantage. This relation, then, is a species of cause and effect. . . ." On the subject of easy transition, see *Treatise*, pp. 507–508, 515, 561, 566.

21. *Treatise*, p. 504, note 1.

22. "Of the Standard of Taste," *Hume's Ethical Writings*, p. 288.

23. Hence the existence of disputes and violence; see *Treatise*, p. 506, note 1: "If we seek a solution of these difficulties in reason and public interest, we never shall find satisfaction; and if we look for it in the imagination, 'tis evident, that the qualities, which operate upon that faculty, run so insensibly and gradually into each other, that 'tis impossible to give them any precise bounds or termination."

24. *Treatise*, p. 568: "But when these titles are mingled and oppos'd in different degrees, they often occasion perplexity; and are less capable of solution from the arguments of lawyers and philosophers, than from the swords of the soldiery."

25. *Treatise*, p. 508, note.

26. *Treatise*, p. 562.

27. *Treatise*, p. 408.

28. *Treatise*, pp. 407–408.

29. *Treatise*, p. 280.

30. *Treatise*, p. 317.

31. *Treatise*, p. 340.

32. *Treatise*, p. 428.

33. *Treatise*, p. 432.

34. David Hume, *An Inquiry Concerning the Principles of Morals*, Charles W. Hendel, ed. and introd. (Indianapolis: Bobbs-Merrill, 1957), pp. 33–34.

35. *Treatise*, pp. 283–284.

36. *Treatise*, p. 555. See also *Treatise*, p. 502: "Justice, in her decisions, never regards the fitness or unfitness of objects to particular persons, but conducts herself by more extensive views."

37. *Treatise*, p. 334.

38. *Treatise*, p. 69.

39. *Treatise*, p. 70.

40. *Treatise*, p. 124.

41. Hume more often uses the term "understanding" with respect to relations of objects; but this is not an absolute rule; see, for example, *Treatise*, p. 166.

42. *Treatise*, p. 84.

43. *Treatise*, p. 89.

44. *Treatise*, p. 89.

45. *Treatise*, p. 179.

46. *Treatise*, p. 130.

47. *Treatise*, pp. 130, 90.

48. *Treatise*, pp. 130–131: "But before it attains this pitch of perfection, it passes thro' several inferior degrees, and in all of them is only to be esteem'd a presumption or probability."

49. *Treatise*, p. 89.

50. *Treatise*, p. 179; *An Enquiry*, pp. 45–46.

51. *Treatise*, p. 179.

52. David Hume, *An Enquiry Concerning Human Understanding* (La Salle: Open Court, 1966), p. 24.

53. *Treatise*, pp. 173–176.

54. There is, however, schematism in mathematics. The idea of a triangle or the idea of a great number does not find in the mind an adequate idea, but only a *power* of producing such an idea: see *Treatise*, pp. 21 and 22. But we will not study this schematism here, because it does not belong to relations, but rather to the general ideas.

55. *Treatise*, p. 265; the italics are mine.

56. *An Enquiry*, p. 39: "It is impossible, therefore, that any arguments from experience can prove this resemblance of the past to the future; since all these arguments are founded on the supposition of that resemblance."

57. *Treatise*, pp. 87–88.

58. *Treatise*, p. 92.

59. *Treatise*, p. 93.

60. *Treatise*, pp. 102–103; see also *Treatise*, p. 114: "[A] belief is an act of the mind arising from custom . . ."; p. 107: ". . . belief arises only from causation."

61. *Treatise*, p. 265.

62. *Treatise*, pp. 88–89.

63. *Treatise*, p. 165.

64. *Treatise*, p. 134.

65. *Treatise*, pp. 169–170, 172.

66. *Treatise*, p. 118.

67. *Treatise*, pp. 110–111.

68. *Treatise*, p. 140.

69. *Treatise*, p. 222.

70. *Treatise*, p. 116.

71. *Treatise*, p. 113.

72. *Treatise*, p. 224.

73. *Treatise*, p. 117.

74. *Treatise*, p. 116.

75. *Treatise*, p. 121.

76. *Treatise*, pp. 121, 122.

77. *Treatise*, p. 630.

78. *Treatise*, p. 123.

79. *Treatise*, p. 630.

80. *Treatise*, pp. 147–148.

81. *Treatise*, p. 148.

82. *Treatise*, p. 147.

83. *Treatise*, p. 149.

84. *Treatise*, p. 133.

85. *Treatise*, p. 136.

86. *Treatise*, p. 140.

87. *Treatise*, p. 149.

88. *Treatise*, p. 150.

89. *Treatise*, pp. 149–150.

90. *Treatise*, p. 173.

91. *Treatise*, p. 631: ". . . the great difference in their feeling proceeds in some measure from reflexion and *general rules*. We observe, that the vigour of conception, which fictions receive from poetry and eloquence, is a circumstance merely accidental."

92. *Treatise*, pp. 147–148.

Chapter Four: God and the World

1. David Hume, *The Natural History of Religion* (London: Adam and Charles Black, 1956), pp. 5–7. Hereafter referred to as NHR.

2. *NHR*, p. 2.

3. *NHR*, p. 10.

4. *NHR*, p. 29.

5. *NHR*, p. 88.

6. "A Dialogue," *Inquiry*, pp. 156–157.

7. *Treatise*, p. 607.

8. *An Enquiry*, p. 120.

9. *Dialogues*, pp. 22–23, 62.

10. *Dialogues*, p. 67. "Why an orderly system may not be spun from the belly as from the brain [?]. . . ."

11. *Dialogues*, X; especially p. 90.

12. *Dialogues*, p. 89.

13. *An Enquiry*, p. 164.

14. *An Enquiry*, p. 124.

15. David Hume, "On Suicide," *Essays. Moral, Political and Literary*, p. 592.

16. "On Suicide," *Essays*, p. 590.

17. *Inquiry*, p. 30.

18. *An Enquiry*, p. 145.

19. *An Enquiry*, p. 59: "and though the powers and forces, by which (nature) is governed, be wholly unknown to us; yet our thoughts and conceptions have still, we find, gone on in the same train with the other works of nature."

20. *Dialogues*, p. 64.

21. *Dialogues*, p. 104.

22. *Dialogues*, p. VII.

23. *Dialogues*, pp. 63–65.

24. *Dialogues*, p. 67.

25. *Treatise*, pp. 194–195.

26. *Treatise*, p. 197.

27. *Treatise*, pp. 196–197. "I am accustom'd to hear such a sound, and see such an object in motion at the same time. I have not receiv'd in this particular instance both these perceptions. These observations are contrary, unless I suppose that the door still remains, and that it was open'd without my perceiving it. . . ."

28. *Treatise*, p. 198.

29. *Treatise*, p. 212.

30. *Treatise*, p. 255. ". . . the objects, which are variable or interrupted, and yet are suppos'd to continue the same, are such only as consist of a succession of parts, connected together by resemblance, contiguity, or causation."

31. *Treatise*, pp. 198–199.

32. *Treatise*, pp. 205–206.

33. *Treatise*, p. 208.

34. *Treatise*, p. 255.

35. *Treatise*, p. 194: "Since all impressions are internal and perishing existences, and appear as such, the notion of their distinct and continu'd existence must arise from a concurrence of some of their qualities with the qualities of the imagination; and since this notion does not extend to all of them, it must arise from certain qualities peculiar to some impressions." See also *Treatise*, p. 255.

36. *Treatise*, p. 187: The skeptic ". . . must assent to the principle concerning the existence of body. . . . Nature has not left this to his choice. . . ."

37. *Treatise*, p. 199.

38. *Treatise*, p. 207: "As to the first question; we may observe, that what we call a *mind*, is nothing but a heap or collection of different perceptions, united together by certain relations, and suppos'd, tho' falsely, to be endow'd with a perfect simplicity and identity. Now as every perception is distinguishable from another, and may be consider'd as separately existent; it evidently follows, that there is no absurdity in separating any particular perception from the mind. . . ."

39. *Treatise*, p. 209: The fiction of a continuous existence and of identity is really false.

40. *Treatise*, p. 215.

41. *Treatise*, p. 218: " 'Tis impossible upon any system to defend either our understanding or senses." Perception to which we attribute continuous existence is what refers us to the senses at this point. See *Treatise*, p. 231: "Thus there is a direct and total opposition betwixt our reason and our senses; or more properly speaking, betwixt those conclusions we form from cause and effect, and those that persuade us of the continu'd and independent existence of body."

42. *Treatise*, p. 215.

43. *Treatise*, pp. 213–214.

44. *Treatise*, p. 211.

45. *Treatise*, p. 215.

46. *Treatise*, pp. 215–216.

47. *Treatise*, p. 212.

48. *Treatise*, p. 215.

49. *Dialogues*, p. 63: Critique of Cosmologies.

50. *Treatise*, pp. 220, 222, 223–224.

51. *Treatise*, pp. 219–225.

52. *Treatise*, p. 226.

53. *Treatise*, pp. 225–231.

54. See *Treatise*, pp. 245–246, for the description of madness.
55. *Treatise*, p. 266.
56. *Treatise*, p. 351.
57. *Treatise*, pp. 225–226.
58. *Treatise*, pp. 267–268.
59. *Treatise*, pp. 181–182.
60. *Treatise*, p. 269.

Chapter Five: Empiricism and Subjectivity

1. *An Enquiry*, p. 83.
2. See chap. 3; see also *Treatise*, pp. 358ff, 585–587.
3. *An Enquiry*, p. 33.
4. *Treatise*, p. 311.
5. "Every thing that enters the mind, being in *reality* as the perception, 'tis impossible any thing shou'd to *feeling* appear different." *Treatise*, p. 190.
6. *Treatise*, p. 18.
7. *Treatise*, p. 234; see also *Treatise*, p. 54: ". . . every idea that is distinguishable, is separable by the imagination; and . . . every idea that is separable by the imagination may be conceived to be separately existent."
8. *Treatise*, p. 244.
9. *Treatise*, pp. 79–81; "Accordingly we shall find upon examination, that every demonstration, which has been produc'd for the necessity of a cause, is fallacious and sophistical." *Treatise*, p. 80.
10. *Treatise*, p. 202.
11. *Treatise*, pp. 192, 226–230.
12. "[A]nd that since the impressions precede their correspondent ideas, there must be some impressions, which without any introduction make their appearance in the soul." *Treatise*, p. 275.
13. *An Enquiry*, p. 21, note: If "by *innate* [we understand] what is original or copied from no precedent perception, then may we assert that all our impressions are innate, and our ideas not innate."
14. *Treatise*, p. 64.
15. *Treatise*, p. 60.
16. "But tho' I have neglected any advantage, which I might have drawn from this topic in explaining the relations of ideas, I am afraid I must here have recourse to it, in order to account for the mistakes that arise from these relations." *Treatise*, p. 60.
17. *Treatise*, p. 207.
18. *Treatise*, p. 207.
19. *Treatise*, p. 27.
20. *Treatise*, p. 27.
21. *Treatise*, p. 27: " 'Tis the same case with the impressions of the senses. . . ."
22. *Treatise*, p. 39.
23. *Treatise*, "Of the Ideas of Space and Time," sections 1, 2, 4.
24. *Treatise*, p. 27.

25. *Treatise*, p. 30.

26. *Treatise*, p. 32.

27. *Treatise*, p. 38.

28. *Treatise*, p. 44.

29. *Treatise*, p. 28: "Nothing can be more minute, than some ideas. . . ."

30. *Treatise*, p. 30.

31. "The only defect in our senses is, that they give us disproportion'd images of things, and represent as minute and uncompounded what is really great and compos'd of a vast number of parts." *Treatise*, p. 28.

32. *Treatise*, "Of the Ideas of Space and Time," 3 and 5.

33. *Treatise*, p. 40.

34. *Treatise*, p. 36.

35. *Treatise*, p. 53.

36. "When we diminish or encrease a relish, 'tis not after the same manner that we diminish or increase any visible object; and when several sounds strike our hearing at once, custom and reflection alone make us form an idea of the degrees of the distance and contiguity of those bodies, from which they are derived." *Treatise*, p. 235.

37. *Treatise*, p. 56. It should be noted that Hume, in this passage as much as in the preceding one, is not raising at all the question about the precise manner in which visual and tactile impressions are distributed as opposed to the distribution of the data from other senses. The reason is that Hume does not seem to be interested in this purely psychological problem.

38. *Treatise*, p. 239.

39. *Treatise*, pp. 34–35.

40. *Treatise*, p. 65.

41. *Treatise*, p. 239.

42. *Treatise*, p. 503. See especially Burke, for whom prescription grounds the right of property.

43. *Treatise*, p. 503.

44. *Treatise*, pp. 508–509.

45. "But as we find by experience, that belief arises only from causation, and that we can draw no inference from one object to another, except they be connected by this relation. . . ." *Treatise*, p. 107.

46. *Treatise*, p. 624.

47. *Treatise*, p. 627.

48. *Treatise*, p. 165.

49. *Treatise*, pp. 102–103.

50. *An Enquiry* p. 47.

51. *An Enquiry*, p 39.

52. *An Enquiry*, pp. 26–27.

53. "The chief exercise of the memory is not to preserve the simple ideas, but their order and position." *Treatise*, p. 9.

54. "The idea of sinking is so closely connected with that of water, and the idea of suffocating with that of sinking, that the mind makes the transition without the assistance of the memory." *Treatise*, p. 104.

55. *Treatise*, pp. 104–105.

56. *Treatise*, pp. 167–168.
57. *An Enquiry*, p. 39. The italics are mine.
58. *Treatise*, Part 3, sect. 6: difference between understanding and imagination, p. 92; difference between causality as a philosophical relation and causality as natural relation, p. 93.
59. *Treatise*, p. 265.
60. We use the term "spontaneity" in view of the following idea: the principles constitute a subject in the mind at the same time that this subject establishes relations among ideas.
61. *Treatise*, p. 60.
62. *Treatise*, p. 37. The italics are mine.
63. *Treatise*, p. 287.
64. *Treatise*, pp. 394–396.
65. *Treatise*, p. 287.
66. *Treatise*, pp. 280–281.
67. *Treatise*, p. 368.
68. *Treatise*, pp. 287 and 395.
69. *Treatise*, p. 69.
70. *Treatise*, p. 46.
71. *Treatise*, p. 239.
72. *Treatise*, p. 65.
73. *Treatise*, p. 74.
74. *Treatise*, p. 13.
75. *Treatise*, p. 11.
76. *Treatise*, pp. 10–11.
77. "Thus distance will be allowed by philosophers to be a true relation, because we acquire an idea of it by the comparing of objects: But in a common way we say, that *nothing can be more distant than such or such things from each other, nothing can have less relation*" *Treatise*, p. 14.
78. *Treatise*, p. 185.
79. *Treatise*, p. 14. The italics are mine.
80. H. Bergson, *Matter and Memory*, N. M. Paul and W. S. Palmer, trs. (New York: Humanities Press, 1978 [1911]), pp. 178–179.
81. ". . . [W]e are only to regard [the uniting principle among ideas] as a gentle force, which commonly prevails, and is the cause why, among other things, languages so nearly correspond to each other." *Treatise*, p. 10.
82. *Treatise*, p. 13. The italics are mine.
83. On the link between circumstances and belief and on the differential significance of the circumstance itself, see *Treatise*, pp. 627–628: "It frequently happens, that when two men have been engag'd in any scene of action, the one shall remember it much better than the other, and shall have all the difficulty in the world to make his companion recollect it. He runs over several circumstances in vain; mentions the time, the place, the company, what was said, what was done on all sides; till at last he hits on some lucky circumstance, that revises the whole, and gives his friend a perfect memory of every thing."
84. *Treatise*, pp. 23–24. The italics are mine.

Chapter Six: Principles of Human Nature

1. *Treatise*, p. 265.
2. *Treatise*, p. 179; the italics are mine.
3. I. Kant, *Critique of Pure Reason*, Norman Kemp Smith, tr. (Toronto: Macmillan, 1929), pp. 132–133: "The Synthesis of Reproduction in Imagination." Hereafter referred to as *Critique*.
4. *Critique*, p. 139: "But as regards the empirical rule of *association*, which we must postulate throughout when we assert that everything in the series of events is so subject to rule that nothing ever happens save in so far as something precedes it on which it universally follows—upon what, I ask, does this rule, as a law of nature, rest? How is this association itself possible? The ground of the possibility of the association of the manifold, so far as it lies in the object, is named the *affinity* of the manifold. I therefore ask, how are we to make comprehensive to ourselves the thoroughgoing affinity of appearances, whereby they stand and *must* stand under unchanging laws?"
5. *Critique*, pp. 145–146: "Since the imagination is itself a faculty of *a priori* synthesis, we assign to it the title, productive imagination. In so far as it aims at nothing but necessary unity in the synthesis of what is manifold in appearance, it may be entitled the transcendental function of imagination."
6. *Critique*, pp. 345–352.
7. *Critique*, p. 142: "This synthetic unity presupposes or includes a synthesis, and if the former is to be *a priori* necessary, the synthesis must also be *a priori*. The transcendental unity of apperception thus relates to the pure synthesis of imagination, as an *a priori* condition of the possibility of all combination of the manifold in one knowledge."
8. *Treatise*, pp. 440–441.
9. *Treatise*, p. 275.
10. *Treatise*, p. 37.
11. *Treatise*, pp. 276–277.
12. *Treatise*, p. 13.
13. *Treatise*, p. 282: ". . . we find in the course of nature, that tho' the effects be many, the principles, from which they arise, are commonly but few and simple, and that 'tis the sign of an unskillful naturalist to have recourse to a different quality, in order to explain every different operation. How much more must this be true with regard to the human mind, which being so confin'd a subject may justly be thought incapable of containing such a monstrous heap of principles. . . ."
14. *Treatise*, pp. 20–21.
15. *Treatise*, pp. 16–17.
16. *Treatise*, p. 25.
17. *Treatise*, p. 13.
18. *Treatise*, p. 17.
19. *Treatise*, p. 265.
20. *Treatise*, p. 169: "This order wou'd not have been excusable, of first examining our inference from the relation before we had explain'd the relation itself, had it been possible to proceed in a different method. But as the nature of the relation depends so much on that of the inference, we

have been oblig'd to advance in this seemingly preposterous manner, and make use of terms before we were able exactly to define them, or fix their meaning."

21. *Treatise*, p. 93.
22. *Treatise*, p. 163.
23. *Treatise*, p. 78: " 'Tis necessary for us to leave the direct survey of this question concerning the nature of that *necessary connexion*, which enters into our idea of cause and effect; and endeavour to find some other questions, the examination of which will perhaps afford a hint, that may serve to clear up the present difficulty."
24. *Treatise*, p. 170.
25. *Treatise*, p. 439.
26. *Treatise*, p. 276.
27. *Treatise*, p. 278.
28. *Treatise*, p. 278.
29. *Treatise*, p. 287.
30. *Treatise*, pp. 438–439.
31. *Treatise*, p. 285.
32. *Treatise*, p. 289.
33. *Treatise*, pp. 304–305.
34. *Treatise*, pp. 438–439.
35. *Treatise*, p. 493.

Conclusion: Purposiveness

1. *Inquiry*, pp. 106–107.
2. *Treatise*, p. 414.
3. *Inquiry*, p. 111.
4. *Treatise*, p. 414.
5. *Treatise*, p. 414.
6. *Inquiry*, p. 108.
7. *Inquiry*, p. 62.
8. *Inquiry*, p. 68.
9. *Treatise*, p. 416.
10. *Inquiry*, p. 105.
11. *Inquiry*, p. 112.
12. *Treatise*, p. 107; see also *An Enquiry*, pp. 55–57.
13. *Inquiry*, p. 108.
14. *Inquiry*, p. 108.
15. *Treatise*, pp. 23–24.
16. *Treatise*, pp. 22–23.
17. *Treatise*, p. 107.
18. *Treatise*, pp. 109–110.
19. *Treatise*, pp. 44–47.
20. *Inquiry*, p. 56, note.
21. *Inquiry*, p. 109.
22. *Inquiry*, p. 64.

23. *Inquiry*, p. 56, note.
24. *Inquiry*, p. 112.
25. *Inquiry*, p. 110.
26. *Treatise*, p. 504.
27. *An Enquiry*, p. 36.
28. *An Enquiry*, p. 59.

INDEX

Institution and drive, 47; and
imagination, 48; and instinct,
47*f*, 49; and law, 45*f*; and
need, 46; system of means, 47;
and utility, 47
Integration, 39*f*; and morality, 36;
and sympathy, 39
Intensity, 13, 16
Intensive schematism, 131
Interest, practical and speculative,
6, 17; rule of, 58; rule and
utility, 49
Invention, 12, 14, 15, 40, 86, 92*f*,
94, 130, 132, 133; and artifice,
86; and legislation, 41; and
morality, 35; political, 50; and
society, 46; and totality, 40, 86

James, William, 99
Justice, 32, 43, 44, 49, 50*f*; and
esteem, 40; and government,
50*f*; and instinct, 44; and
passions, 43, 44; not a principle
of nature, 40; scheme of, 36;
single, 50*f*; and totality, 49

Kafka: Toward a Minor Literature,
1, 136*n*9
Kant, ix, 75, 99, 105, 107, 109,
110*f*, 114, 119
Knowing subject, 120
Knowledge, 71, 132; and ethics,
21-36; extensive, 127; and
mental activity, 127; and
morality, 68; and passions, 6,
129; and transcendence, 28, 34

Lack and society, 46
Language and belief, 70
Laporte, Jean, 92, 139*n*35
Law and institution, 45*f*
Lecercle, Jean-Jacques, 1
Legislation and invention, 41
Leibniz, Gottfried Wilhelm, 1,
11, 107; -effect, 13; -series, 13
Limited Inc., 137*n*36

The Logic of Sense, 1, 3, 4, 12,
136*nn*10, 11, 19, 20
Lucretius, 4

Madness, 83, 84
Martelaere, Patricia de, 138*n*53
Memory, 94*f*
Merleau Ponty, Maurice, 4
Mind, 7, 59, 87, 88, 91, 96, 98,
99, 119*f*, 123, 124, 127, 132;
activity and passivity, 119;
affections of, 21; collection of
ideas, 22; collection of
impressions and ideas, 132;
constitution of, 31; and
delirium, 23, 83; and fancy,
83; and human nature, 59, 92;
imagination and ideas, 22; and
madness, 3, 22; not the
representation of nature, 88;
passivitiy of, 26; and principles
of human nature, 15; product
of the powers of nature, 17;
quantity, 90, schematism of,
127; and self, 31; and space,
91; and subject, 7, 23, 26, 31,
112, 119; tendency of, 25; and
time, 91; and transcendence,
29
Minoritarian discourse, 2
Modern French Philosophy, 3
Morality, 124, 126; and exclusion,
35; general rules and justice,
32; and inference, 35; and
integration, 36; and invention,
35; and knowledge, 68; and
nature, 40; and politics, 41;
and reason, 123, 124; and
totality, 40
Moral obligation, 42
Moral schematism, 131
Moral world, artificial totality, 41

The Natural History of Religion,
146*nn*1, 2, 3, 4, 5
Natural relations, 114*f*, 116, 123
Nature, 6; and artifice, 43; and

European Perspectives
A Series in Social Thought and Cultural Criticism
Lawrence D. Kritzman, Editor